ELEPHANTS

ELEPHANTS

THE DECIDING DECADE

EDITED BY RONALD ORENSTEIN

INTRODUCTION BY RICHARD LEAKEY

PHOTOGRAPHY BY BRIAN BECK

CONTRIBUTORS:

JEHESKEL SHOSHANI

PEREZ OLINDO

DAVID WESTERN

IAN REDMOND

SIERRA CLUB BOOKS

San Francisco

For our children, who will inherit the wildlife we save
and, especially, for Randy and Jenny

R.O.

Page 2:
*Elephants and people meet
at close quarters in some
areas. This elephant stops
just short of camping gear
in Chobe National Park,
Botswana.*

Pages 4-5:
*Four Chobe bulls demonstrate
the stages of taking a drink.
Like the animal in the fore-
ground, elephants often
insert the trunk tip well into
the mouth when drinking, to
avoid spilling water. In times
of drought they can do the
reverse — drawing water
from a pouch in their throats
to bathe their skin.*

Page 8:
*Rock paintings, or picto-
graphs, provide evidence of
man's long fascination with
the African elephant. These
ancient paintings were made
by Bushmen on the red
granite cliffs of Dombos-
hawa, Zimbabwe.*

The Sierra Club, founded in 1892 by John Muir, has devoted itself to the study and protection of the earth's scenic and ecological resources—mountains, wetlands, woodlands, wild shores and rivers, deserts and plains. The publishing program of the Sierra Club offers books to the public as a nonprofit educational service in the hope that they may enlarge the public's understanding of the Club's basic concerns. The point of view expressed in each book, however, does not necessarily represent that of the Club. The Sierra Club has some sixty chapters coast to coast, in Canada, Hawaii, and Alaska. For information about how you may participate in its programs to preserve wilderness and the quality of life, please address inquiries to Sierra Club, 730 Polk Street, San Francisco, CA 94109.

Library of Congress Cataloging-in-Publication Data

Elephants: the deciding decade / edited by Ronald Orenstein.
p.   cm.
Includes bibliographical references and index.
ISBN 0-87156-565-X
1. African elephant.   2. Wildlife conservation — Africa.
I. Orenstein. Ronald I. (Ronald Isaac), 1946–
QL737.P98E45   1991
333.95'9 — dc20   91-15254
                                                        CIP

Book design by Andrew Smith

Printed and bound in Italy by Nuovo Istituto Italiano d'Arti Grafiche - Bergamo

10 9 8 7 6 5 4 3 2 1

CONTENTS

A LETTER TO THE READER

The Department of Wildlife in Tanzania, working in close cooperation with the International Wildlife Coalition, has established a scholarship fund to benefit the children of rangers and game scouts as an incentive for exemplary service. We in the Department of Wildlife have been very much encouraged by this generous initiative by the donors and supporters of the International Wildlife Coalition on behalf of Tanzania's wildlife. I am delighted to learn that 100 percent of the royalties from the sale of Elephants *will be donated to the IWC Scholarship Fund.*

IWC has undertaken to provide, this first year, a total of U.S. $15,000 to fund the initiative. The Department has announced the scholarship plan and called upon its officers to inform all game scouts and rangers. We intend to award thirty scholarships worth TAS 100,000 each to scouts and rangers whose dedication and achievement in anti-poaching work has been outstanding. The award money will then be available to pay for those rangers' children's education, provided, too, that they (the children) excelled in class.

We hope that this scheme will act as a powerful incentive for more discipline and lead to more success with work aimed at conservation of the African elephant and other endangered species. We trust, too, that other donors will find a way of participating and ensuring the success of this pioneering work. On behalf of the staff of the Department of Wildlife, I pay tribute to this demonstration of good will by the International Wildlife Coalition, and hope its success will augur well for the future.

COSTA A. MLAY
DIRECTOR, WILDLIFE DIVISION,
MINISTRY OF LANDS, NATURAL RESOURCES AND TOURISM,
UNITED REPUBLIC OF TANZANIA

PREFACE

ON OCTOBER 18, 1989, AFTER ONE OF THE MOST INTENSIVE WORLD-WIDE CONSERVATION campaigns ever conducted, the delegates at the Seventh Conference of the Parties to the Convention on International Trade in Endangered Species of Wild Fauna and Flora, or CITES, voted to transfer the African elephant to the treaty's Appendix I. That action effectively ended the international ivory trade. In the ensuing months, the price of ivory has fallen to rock-bottom levels and the poaching that was killing three hundred elephants every day has practically ground to a halt. Years of effort fighting a crisis that was overwhelming the conservation resources of many African countries had suddenly — contrary to the predictions of a number of doom-saying economists and wildlife managers — borne fruit. Rarely has such a massive threat to a species' survival evaporated so quickly once proper action was finally taken.

Nineteen eighty-nine was the year of hope for the African elephant. The 1990s will be its deciding decade. What we do in the next few years will determine whether the greatest land animal on earth starts its recovery after years of rampant slaughter, or slides once more towards extinction.

The five extraordinary people whose words you will read in these pages have devoted many years of their lives to saving the African elephant. Through science, politics, law enforcement, education, activism and the restoration of Africa's cultural heritage, they have — each in his own way — played central roles in the war against the ivory trade. They have written this book to enlist you in that continuing struggle, to inform you about its roots, and to make you care, as they do, about the elephant and all that it means to Africa.

For the elephant is not safe yet. True, poaching appears to have been almost eliminated, but that "almost" means that some eight thousand elephants a year are still dying at the poacher's hand. Although that is less than 10 percent of pre-ban levels, it is too high for anyone who loves elephants. Furthermore, the ivory poachers could come back in force. The traders who were growing fat on the slaughter of elephants are not foolish

An elephant emerges from the Chobe River, Chobe National Park, Botswana.

11

men, and if there is an opportunity to revive such a lucrative trade they will surely use it.

The wildlife of Africa, including the African elephant, still faces many other threats: population pressure, the loss of habitat, political uncertainties and desertification as overused, deforested lands decline into barren wastes. Elephants in the Gourma region of Mali, for example, have been dying of thirst as silt from the expanding desert clogs their water holes. In short, all the gains we have made could yet be lost. The African elephant is still at our mercy.

It was not always so. Once, the African elephant ranged from the shores of the Mediterranean to the temperate heathlands of the Cape of Good Hope. Scientists estimate that five to ten million elephants roamed across Africa, on desert and mountain, over the broad savannahs, and through the shadows of the tropical rainforest. Their herds trekked in great migrations across thousands of miles, following the rains. They changed the land itself as they passed, uprooting trees, trampling brush, even — as Ian Redmond speculates later in this book — excavating deep caves in mountain cliffs.

Man began to change this picture centuries ago, as waves of traders and conquerors invaded Africa in search of its slaves, its ebony and spices, and its greatest luxury, ivory. The elephants of North Africa were killed off in medieval times. During the eighteenth and early nineteenth centuries, as European colonists spread outwards from the Cape, elephants disappeared over much of the southern end of the continent. Another ivory rush, peaking around the end of the last century, reduced the elephant herds of West Africa to tattered remnants.

By the early years of this century, the conservation movement had begun to develop in Europe and America. Big game hunters travelling in Africa became concerned about the fate of the elephant, and colonial governments passed laws controlling the ivory trade. Perhaps more importantly, after the First World War the price of ivory, and the demand for it, fell. In Central, Eastern and Southern Africa, the herds began to recover.

By 1966, when I visited the continent, the problem people were talking about in East Africa was not elephant decline, but elephant overpopulation. Crowded into the reserves that were becoming, even then, the only remaining patches of natural habitat, elephants were demolishing the forests in places like Murchison Falls National Park in Uganda. I remember having to walk carefully at night, even in the tourist compounds, to avoid blundering into groups of curious elephants.

A few years later, the picture began to change again, and change drastically. The colonial programs of wildlife conservation, based as they were on European, not African, values and privileges, came under attack as newly independent states began to forge their own destinies. Demand for ivory surpassed pre-1914 levels, particularly in a now affluent Japan where ivory name-seals, or *hanko*, had become a status item. Its price, which had hovered around U.S. $5.45 a kilo for years, jumped to $7.44 in 1970. By 1978 it had reached $74.42, and by the beginning of 1989 — the height of the ivory crisis — it had reached as much as $300–$400 a kilo in Japan and $150 a kilo in Africa. Ivory had become not just a valuable commodity, but a well-nigh irresistible one to many of Africa's poor.

At the same time, the means to acquire this fabulous source of wealth fell increasingly into their hands. The civil wars and wars of liberation that

12

plagued Africa throughout the sixties attracted international arms dealers. Thousands of semi-automatic weapons — AK-47s, Kalashnikovs and the like — poured into Africa. According to the U.S. Arms Control and Disarmament Agency, arms imports to Africa increased (in real terms) from U.S. $500 million in 1971 to $4,500 million in 1980. When law and order broke down — as it did in Uganda and elsewhere — it was a simple matter for many of these weapons to find their way into the hands of ivory poachers.

The poachers, of course, could not act alone. They were, in fact, at the bottom of an economic pyramid dominated by millionaire dealers. These kingpins of the ivory trade lived, for the most part, in Hong Kong. They used their wealth and ingenuity to bribe complaisant officials, circumvent anti-poaching laws, move the poached tusks out of Africa, and funnel the bulk of their vast ivory profits into Swiss bank accounts.

The extent of their deviousness was revealed in a blistering report published in 1989 by a dauntless, independent band of undercover conservationists. The Environmental Investigation Agency sent its troops into ivory factories in Dubai (where they hid in packing crates, snapping pictures), to the African outports and into the dens of the major dealers in Hong Kong. EIA's report told of forged permits, bribery and shenanigans at every level. Hong Kong, for example, had a law banning the import of "raw" — that is, uncarved — ivory. To circumvent the law, the smugglers

The elephant can earn far more money for Africa as a living tourist attraction than as a source of ivory. These tourists are visiting Mana Pools National Park, Zimbabwe, a spot popular with both travellers and locals.

13

opened carving factories in the United Arab Emirates and Bangladesh. There the poached tusks were whittled a bit before being shipped to Hong Kong, where skilled carvers cut the ivory into finished products.

No animal could withstand such a barrage of forces. Elephant populations went into free fall. By 1989 African elephant numbers were down to 625,000 or so—half of what they had been only a decade earlier. Faced with the imminent extinction of the elephant, the international community was forced to act. The tool it used, or tried to use, was CITES — the treaty under which the ivory ban was finally passed.

CITES works on a system of permits. The plants or animals affected by CITES are listed in three appendices. Appendix I includes species threatened with extinction which are or may be affected by trade. When a species is placed on Appendix I, it can only be traded internationally if permits are issued both by the importing and by the exporting country. More to the point, species on Appendix I cannot be traded for primarily commercial purposes. Appendices II and III include species that are not necessarily endangered, but that bear watching in case trade does start to affect their survival. Such species need only an export permit and can be traded for commercial purposes.

The African elephant was placed on Appendix III in 1976, and shortly thereafter was transferred to Appendix II. All through the 1980s, it was clear that elephant populations were dropping fast. However, it took a long time for the scientific community to realize that poaching, rather than habitat loss or other factors, was the major culprit. Furthermore, the ivory trade was worth a lot of money. Some African countries like Zimbabwe, which still had healthy elephant populations, were culling elephants to prevent overcrowding, selling the ivory, and using the profits to fund conservation programs within their borders. This legal trade amounted to only about 10 percent of the world's ivory supply, but the countries engaged in it were unwilling to give it up. So the African elephant stayed on Appendix II, although its cousin, the Asian elephant, was already on Appendix I.

As long as legal ivory was available, the illegal trade could flourish. For years the CITES member states struggled to control the poachers while permitting the legal trade to continue. They tried marking schemes, quota schemes, computer-tracking schemes. Nothing worked. Once ivory was carved, no one could tell the legal from the illegal, and the permits that made trade possible were easily forged, stolen or re-used. The price of ivory continued to skyrocket, and the ivory traders who dealt in poached goods—mostly in Hong Kong—found ways to get around every scheme that CITES could devise.

Finally, the world woke up to what was happening. In May 1989, after pressure from conservationists and animal protectionists worldwide, Canada, the United States, the European Community, Australia and other importing countries banned the commercial importation of ivory. That October the CITES member states met in Lausanne, Switzerland. I attended as an observer for the International Wildlife Coalition. After a stormy two-week session the member states voted to transfer the African elephant from Appendix II to Appendix I. That transfer came into effect officially on January 18, 1990, although many countries had already put it into place immediately after the meeting.

The ban was not achieved without compromise. The original pro-

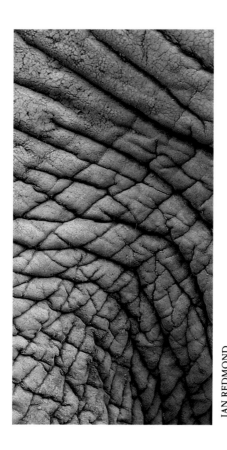

IAN REDMOND

The wrinkled skin of an elephant varies in thickness, but may be over an inch thick in some places.

A close-up view of an elephant's eye.

IAN REDMOND

posal had been unacceptable to some African countries. The Southern African countries, led by Zimbabwe whose representatives objected strenuously to any suggestion that the African elephant was truly endangered, wanted a special exemption for themselves to continue their legal trade. Some West African countries complained that Southern Africa was getting special treatment, and other countries feared that if the elephant was placed on Appendix I it would stay there, because of the wording of the CITES rules, even if the herds recovered. The ban was finally accepted with an amendment introduced by Somalia, one of the original proponents. The amendment contains rules under which a country can apply to have the ban lifted for its territories. Under this system — using a plan first drawn up by Ruth Mace of the Ivory Trade Review Group, Mark Stanley Price of the African Wildlife Foundation and myself—a country can ask to have a panel of experts visit it to survey its elephant populations, its antipoaching controls and the degree to which it can control ivory smuggling through its territories. If the country receives a satisfactory assessment, the CITES members may allow it to resume trading in ivory. Once this plan had been accepted, a working group, ably chaired by Perez Olindo, met to develop the details under which the new rules would operate. This system was designed to be fair to all African countries, and, frankly, without it I believe that the ban would never have been passed.

What did all this mean? It meant that after January 18, 1990 (and earlier than that for countries passing their own bans), ivory, other elephant products or living elephants could not be imported or exported from one CITES party to another for commercial purposes. Personal effects and hunting trophies could be carried across borders with the proper paperwork, as could scientific specimens, zoo animals and some other exceptions. However, if ivory had been imported into a country before the ban, it could be sold there. To make the situation more confusing, any ivory imported either before 1976, when the African elephant was first placed on the treaty, or before a country joined CITES, could be traded as "pre-convention" ivory.

And there are loopholes. Over a hundred countries belong to CITES, but a few important trading nations such as Taiwan and South Korea do not. Five African countries (Zimbabwe, Malawi, Botswana, South Africa and Zambia, who felt unable to accept a ban even under the new rules) and two importing countries (China and Great Britain) entered reservations to the Appendix I listing. This is a perfectly legal, although hardly admirable, procedure under the treaty. It allows any state, within ninety days of a vote, to simply announce that it has no intention of being bound by the decision of the parties. As a result, for those seven countries the African elephant remained on Appendix II.

The British reservation was a special one, though. It applied only to Hong Kong and was intended to last only six months. Its purpose was to allow Hong Kong to export some of the over six hundred tons of ivory that it had stockpiled. Nonetheless the British reservation aroused the fury of conservationists worldwide. Britain had been one of the chief supporters of the Appendix I listing in the first place, and had even introduced a resolution urging countries to ignore the ninety-day waiting period after the meeting and put the ban in place at once. But Prime Minister Margaret Thatcher was having trouble with officials in Hong Kong for reasons that had nothing to do with the ivory trade. Despite her government's stated policy, and the fact that the parties at the Lausanne meeting had rejected a plea by Hong Kong to be allowed to sell off its stockpile (which consisted largely, if not entirely, of poached ivory), she ordered the reservation to appease the colony's business community.

Ivory, therefore, can still be sold legally, and the smugglers still have routes that they could follow. The world ivory trade has collapsed anyway — not because of the ban alone, though it certainly was a tremendous help, but because people like you have refused to buy ivory. In most parts of the world today, ivory — which fetched hundreds of dollars a kilo only a few months before the CITES ban — is not selling at any price. Two-thirds of India's two thousand ivory carvers are out of business. Hong Kong was unable, during its six-month grace period, to sell off more than a small part of its stockpile. Ivory-carving factories in China are practically bankrupt. In fact, in late 1990 China gave up the struggle and withdrew its reservation, effective January 11, 1991.

But the battle is not over. Elephant populations are still only half of what they were a decade ago. East Africa has lost 85 percent of its elephants. Even if all of the threats the elephant faces are removed or held in check, it will be decades before the herds in places like East Africa can build up their numbers again. Africa needs our awareness and our help.

The ivory traders and the poachers that supply them have not gone away. Plans are already in the works to attack the trade ban at the next CITES meeting, to be held in Kyoto, Japan, in March 1992. Dealers are searching for new ivory customers in Asia, especially in countries like South Korea that do not belong to CITES. In Vietnam, Laos and Thailand ivory jewelry has recently become popular. The ivory they use comes from the African elephant's much rarer cousin, the Asian elephant. Poaching has never been much of a problem in Asia, but now that African ivory is hard to obtain the small Laotian population of Asian elephants has come under the gun. If the trade ban is lifted, though, you can be sure that African ivory will start flowing into this new market. In the expectation that the ban will not last, dealers and poachers are stockpiling ivory in anticipation of the day that the profits from this terrible trade rise once again. We cannot afford to be complacent.

Tusks cover the ground at a legal ivory auction in Harare, Zimbabwe, in 1986 — before the ivory ban. Zimbabwe and other southern African countries opposed the ban, claiming the profits from sales like this one were needed to fund their wildlife conservation programs. The dark band around each tusk marks the point at which it emerged from the elephant's face.

There is an important lesson that the African elephant, and the fight to save it, can teach us. That is that efforts to help rescue a wild species — even if they are motivated, for many of us, solely by the awe, fascination and pure love that a magnificent animal can inspire — can have direct economic and environmental benefits for people. The words of Richard Leakey, David Western and others in this book tell the tale. Without the African elephant, Africa would become impoverished, not just in terms of direct revenues from wildlife tourism and other sources, but in terms of the very land itself, land that the elephant helps to shape and diversify. When fortunes no longer have to be spent to control gangs of poachers, they can be used to provide the social benefits that Africans desperately need. By saving the African elephant we may be helping to save Africa itself.

That is the reason for this book — that, and the opportunity to celebrate, in words and pictures, this truly wonderful and awe-inspiring animal.

18

INTRODUCTION

RICHARD LEAKEY

WHEN I WAS ASKED BY PRESIDENT DANIEL ARAP MOI OF KENYA TO TAKE OVER THE directorship of Kenya's Department of Wildlife, it came as an unexpected request. It's a job for which I have had no training, and a job that is very complex, involving biology, ecology, conservation, economics, politics and international affairs, not to mention stamina. I wondered, "Why me? Surely there is somebody else more deserving of these troubles?"

One of the things that I have discovered, to my surprise, is that conservation is as political and as tendentious and as difficult as anything I have ever dealt with before. I remember well being dismayed and discouraged about the politics in anthropology. People used to say it had to be one of the most politicized and difficult fields because it's concerned with humanity; well, conservation is worse. I don't even get out of the office any more. At least when I ran the National Museums of Kenya, I could sometimes get away to see elephants.

I doubted whether it would be possible to turn the situation around in Kenya in the time we had left. We had seen a rapid increase in the number of elephants being killed by poachers. We had inadequate funding for effective park management, and the lawlessness in our national parks showed that we had lost control of them. The roads upon which the antipoaching forces were to travel were pretty well gone as a result of erosion and lack of maintenance. The vehicles that had been provided over the years for antipoaching and patrol operations had ceased to function. The men charged with the responsibility of looking after our wildlife were ill-equipped, ill-clothed and underpaid. We had read for week after week of the success of these incredible gangs of poachers that swept into Kenya, rampaged through our parks and slaughtered our elephants, yet never a one was taken to court and effectively prosecuted. There were reports of corruption everywhere.

The President of Kenya gave me a mandate, and the authority to carry it out. It was made absolutely clear to me that the poaching had to stop. The killing of elephants had to stop. The threat to our tourists had to stop,

With dust on their backs and mud on their feet, a cow and juveniles walk along the edge of the Chobe River, Botswana.

19

and the parks had to be put back on their feet and made to work again.

Kenya is a poor country, and depends heavily upon its number one industry, tourism. Wildlife—centered on the elephant—is the foundation of our tourist industry. Some months before I was appointed I likened the slaughter of elephants to an act of deliberate economic sabotage. I queried in the press whether we would tolerate saboteurs who burned down our coffee plantations and tea estates in the way that we apparently tolerated those who were destroying our elephants.

The situation facing elephants today is far better than it has been for a long time. We had been losing three elephants a day in the national parks, and had been doing so for a number of years. Since May 15, 1989, when many Western nations banned the commercial import of ivory, that loss has declined dramatically.

We believe that in 1989 we lost fewer than three hundred elephants. In fact, from April 1989 until April 1990 the figure was less than two hundred. With the exception of an incursion that took place in July 1990, when we lost eleven elephants on Mount Elgon to a group that came across from Uganda, only fourteen elephants are known to have been killed by poachers in the first part of that year. Only thirty-three elephants had been illegally killed as of October 30, 1990. This is remarkable considering the level of slaughter that we had seen just a year before. Given the national population of about eighteen thousand elephants, and given the likelihood of reproduction and the recruitment rates—that is, the rates at which new animals are added to the population—that we now believe to exist, Kenya's elephants may actually be on the increase for the first time in many, many years.

We now have aerial surveillance, foot patrols, ground patrols. We are opening up areas that had long since ceased to function as viewing sites, and we are beginning to see a change, a change that will gain momentum.

We have, in the past, had incidents where tourists were robbed and threatened—indeed, some innocent tourists met their deaths in our country. The perpetrators of those vile crimes have been brought to justice, and today I believe it is fair and correct to say that the parks of Kenya are safer than they have been for the last ten or fifteen years.

There has been progress in reestablishing Kenya's Wildlife Service. The Government of Kenya saw fit to change its legislation, and to provide an opportunity for the Wildlife Service to be run not as a government department, with the inevitable bureaucracies that government departments develop, but as a state corporation—a corporation that is owned by the government and possesses a Board of Directors appointed by the government. Once established, however, the corporation is run as a business. In this system, we can now pay men and women proper salaries for the jobs they do, discipline them if they don't do the jobs they should, charge a fee for admission into our parks and put the money from that revenue directly into conservation. We can evaluate long-term strategies to ensure that there will be wildlife not only for tourists and the people of Kenya today, but also for tomorrow and beyond.

When I began, I would not have believed that it would be possible to turn the situation around. I gave Kenya's elephants no more than two years in terms of their capacity to sustain themselves on any viable basis. The fact that we are no longer losing large numbers of elephants suggests to me that I was wrong, and that we can after all ensure that the survival

JONATHAN SCOTT / PLANET EARTH PICTURES

of the Kenya population is guaranteed.

What we have shown is that poaching can be stopped. Poaching can be stopped both at our end, by dealing with the poachers, and at the other end by dealing with the demand for ivory. We want to spread that message, that technique, that experience. If we can show that a ghastly, devastating situation can be turned around in a matter of years, then there will be hope for others. If we can do it, others can do it. There is just enough time.

We have seen a change in the attitude to ivory. Many of you will remember the decision by Kenya — in an action undertaken by our President — to set fire to about twelve tons of ivory in July 1989. That twelve tons represented approximately two thousand magnificent animals, animals whose ivory had been obtained from poachers' hoards confiscated by security patrols. That stock of two thousand animals' worth of ivory was a mere fraction of the ivory that we knew to be in Kenya and to be moving out of Kenya, and a mere fraction of the ivory that had been moving out of Kenya in the past.

In an action of tremendous symbolic importance, twelve tons of confiscated ivory burn to ash in a fire set by Kenya's President Daniel Arap Moi in Nairobi National Park.

Our decision to burn it was ridiculed by some. They said, "Why burn it? Why not sell it? You're desperate for money, you have no vehicles, your aircraft are broken down, your roads are unfinished, your bridges are collapsing, your men have no boots and you have no ammunition for your guns and you're burning three million dollars' worth of ivory. Are you crazy?"

We said, "Perhaps we are crazy, but we don't think so." We believed that as long as there was a market, the poachers would continue to poach. In Africa people are desperate for a livelihood. We do not have social welfare. We do not have high salaries. Our people have few opportunities to send their children to school, college and university. If there is a commodity such as ivory that has a high value, even though we might destroy one gang of poachers, another gang will take its place. The only way to take the pressure off the elephant was to destroy the market.

To destroy the market, we had to get the attention of the world. In particular, we had to get the attention of consumers — people like yourselves, who are used to being influenced by advertising campaigns, who have money to buy souvenirs and trinkets. We could not afford to take on a public relations firm to make our statement. We believed that setting fire to the ivory and destroying it would demonstrate our commitment to the elephant's cause. We could hardly say to people in affluent countries, "Don't buy ivory," while we were still selling ivory. We felt that such a double standard would be inappropriate.

So we burned our ivory, and the world noticed. A few months later the CITES ban on the ivory trade was passed, and, contrary to what some economists had said, the price of ivory began to fall.

Ivory today is worth at least 75 percent less than it was at the time of the fire. Prices in Africa have fallen as low as four to five dollars a kilo. In Kenya and in Tanzania — the two countries that have probably suffered more than any others from the devastation of poaching — ivory has been found abandoned. In late 1989 a Tanzanian patrol found large quantities of poached ivory in the Selous Game Reserve, which had been thrown away. We have had similar reports in Kenya, of our patrols finding ivory no longer concealed but simply abandoned to the elements, the people who put it there having long since fled from our parks, and from our country.

I don't believe that we can yet afford to congratulate ourselves. Although a particular battle has been won, the war has not yet been won. Constant vigilance is required.

I believe the current situation reflects the fact that in many parts of the world people no longer buy ivory. I believe people no longer buy ivory partly because it has become socially unacceptable to do so. Dozens of organizations worldwide have worked hard to achieve this change in attitude. Their work has led to a popular revulsion toward ivory, and that revulsion has resulted in the reduction of poaching to its present level in Kenya and, probably, in the rest of Africa.

It's not just that we now have better guns and better men and more money. We do. But if the price of ivory were still high, we would still be fighting a battle a day. Instead of fighting, we are painting houses, repairing roofs, fixing roads and rebuilding bridges. There's virtually no poaching activity in the field at the moment. I think this is true in Tanzania. I think it's true in Uganda. I think it's true in Somalia and Ethiopia. It's certainly

true in Central Africa. And although the price of ivory varies throughout the world, it is way, way down and there are great stocks of ivory that cannot be sold.

This is not Kenya's achievement alone, but an achievement of all mankind. I'm glad that, working together in a common cause, we've done it.

But we have to keep doing it, and to keep doing it we need elephant books such as the one you are holding in your hand. We need Elephant talk, we need Ele-friends, we need Ele-children.

We need your support, whether that takes the form of money, or of signatures on petitions, or what you teach your children or say to your dinner guests.

This book, and your purchase of it, is further evidence that people do care. If you care, and we stop the ivory trade once and for all, the slaughter of these wonderful animals will cease to be a fact. We will move to a new world where the elephant will have a chance for survival in its ancient home on the African continent.

A large bull strides towards the photographer in the Zambesi Valley, Zimbabwe. The tears in its ears — perhaps the result of an encounter with a thorn tree — are a common sight on adults, and can be used to help recognize individuals.

Following pages:
The vleis — the marshland — of Elim Dune, Namibia, are home to the remarkable desert elephants, a small population that ekes out an existence in this arid land.

ELEPHANT COUNTRY

Almost all of Africa was once elephant country. Even today, as humans continue to drive them out of many of their former haunts, African elephants can still be found in a broader range of habitats than almost any other large mammal. From the deserts of Namibia and the Sahara through grassland, savannah and woodland to the rainforests of Central Africa and the chilly cloud forests of the mountain peaks, the elephant is not only a dweller in the land but a molder of its shape, clearing vegetation, dispersing seeds, and creating habitat for other wild species.

These open marshy grass-lands on Zimbabwe's Fothergill Island form part of the home range of this bull. Ivory is a fairly elastic material and does not break easily; perhaps this one was injured in a fight with another bull, or misjudged his leverage while trying to debark a tree.

Accompanied by a flock of cattle egrets (Bubulcus ibis)*, elephants cross a savannah in the Zambesi Valley, Zimbabwe, through tall grass dotted with thorn trees and termite mounds—perhaps the most "typical" elephant country in most people's imagination.*

This stony ground in Etosha Park, Namibia, offers little to elephants; here a herd of cows and calves crosses it, single file, along one of their regular trails.

The cycle of dry and wet seasons in Africa, which can see a river like the Sand River in Mana Pools National Park, Zimbabwe, turn into a dry bed, governs the long migrations of African elephants—or at least did, before human settlement cut off many of their migration routes.

Baboons watch as a herd passes through the woodlands of the Zambesi Valley, Zimbabwe.

Desertification—the expansion of Africa's deserts, like these at Sossovlei, Namibia—is a growing environmental problem. Although elephants do live in desert habitats like these, they are already dying of thirst in Mali, where available water holes are becoming clogged with Saharan sand.

Scattered clumps of yellow melons provide succulent food for Namibia's famed desert elephants.

This gathering of a bull elephant, Chacma baboons (Papio ursinus) *and impala* (Aepyceros melampus) *in Chobe National Park, Botswana, may not be coincidental. The elephant's acute sense of smell, the impalas' keen hearing or the baboons' sharp eyes and ability to climb trees for a better view may provide the first warning of danger.*

A herd of cows mills about a woodland clearing in the Zambesi Valley, Zimbabwe. The tree in the background has been damaged by animals—possibly by elephants.

A big tusker, the tip of one tusk broken off, eyes the photographer in the woodlands of the Zambesi Valley, Zimbabwe. The tall earthen column in the background is a termite mound.

A bull pauses in the woodlands of the Zambesi Valley, Zimbabwe.

A grand old baobab tree (Adansonia digitata) *in Gonarezhou National Park, Zimbabwe. An African legend attributes its strange shape to the anger of the gods, who uprooted it and stuck it back into the ground upside down.*

The relatively soft wood of a baobab provides elephants like this young bull in Gonarezhou National Park, Zimbabwe, with a source of vitamins and minerals, and they will go to extremes to get at it.

Covered with mud from his wallow, this thirtyish bull is both protected against insect bites and shielded from the sun's heat. He was photographed in the Zambesi Valley, Zimbabwe.

Elephants are most active in the early morning and the late afternoon, like these two bulls on Zimbabwe's Fothergill Island.

A distant, solitary bull crosses the grasslands of Fothergill Island, Zimbabwe. Fothergill is a man-made island formed when the Kariba Dam created Lake Kariba; it is named after Rupert Fothergill, whose "Operation Noah" saved many animals from the rising waters. Several bulls live there permanently; breeding herds swim to the island in the dry season.

39

LAST OF A NOBLE LINE

JEHESKEL SHOSHANI

WE FOLLOWED A PATH THAT SNAKED DEEP INTO THE FOREST, MARKED WITH ELEPHANT footprints and freshly broken branches. The footprints led to a sheer volcanic rock wall covered with water plants. A tiny spring oozed out of the rock, where birds came to drink. Suddenly, a bushbuck ran into the thicket, and a few minutes later we saw the unmistakable head of the most famous wild elephant in the world. Ahmed flapped his ears, raised his trunk and trumpeted softly. We could clearly see his distinctive long eyelashes and sunken cheeks. His huge ears were marked with long tears. However, it was his tusks that astonished us: there was something special about those tusks, not only their ten-foot (3 m) length, but also their curvature and symmetry. As he raised and lowered his head, the tips of his tusks touched the forest floor.

Ahmed started to walk backwards, feeling the solid ground underneath his feet just as a blind person would use a cane to test the surface before stepping. He started with his right hind leg, cautiously and gently tapping the ground a short distance behind him. Once the ground was "tested," he rested his right hind leg backwards and repeated the process with the right foreleg, left hind leg and finally with the left foreleg. While he was inching his way backwards and downhill in the forest, he was constantly looking at us, his head and trunk making slight movements. After about ten minutes of slow maneuvering downhill with his head facing us uphill, he disappeared into the forest.

I was a tourist when I saw Ahmed in July 1973 in his home in the Marsabit Game Reserve of Kenya — a land of forests, mountains, hills and valleys, rising like an island-oasis in the middle of the desert. Before my visit, I had heard many strange tales about him: how he was guarded by special "Askaris," soldier-elephants that escorted him through the forest; how, fearing that his three hundred pounds (130 kg) of ivory would attract poachers, five thousand people had written to the East African Wildlife Society on Ahmed's behalf; how President Mzee Jomo Kenyatta had issued a special decree to protect him, and assigned a team of human soldiers to

The trunk and tusks of this female elephant are its most useful tools. The African elephant's trunk is banded with ridged rings, or annuli.

There are two forms, or subspecies, of African ele- phant: the forest elephant (Loxodonta africana cyclotis) of the Central African rain- forests, and the more wide- spread bush or savannah elephant (L. a. africana), like this mature bull dozing in Kenya's Amboseli National Park. They differ in many ways from their Asian cous- ins: for example, their ears are larger, and their backs are swayed. Notice how the tusks curve together in the front, protecting the trunk.

track his whereabouts around the clock. But seeing him alive was a spiri- tual experience, a turning point in my life. My heart pounded; I grasped my friend's wrist and squeezed it so hard that I startled him. It was at that moment, I believe, that I decided to devote my life to the study of elephants.

The two living species of elephants—Ahmed and his kind, the African elephant (*Loxodonta africana*), and the Asian elephant (*Elephas maximus*) —are the end points of over fifty million years of evolutionary history. I have spent many years studying that record. My studies have taken me to the Fayum basin of Egypt where, some fifty to sixty million years ago, lived the pig-sized mammals from which evolved elephant-like creatures — the proboscideans, named for their proboscis or trunk. I have dug for the bones of the mammoths and mastodons that roamed the earth at the end of the ice age. I would love to have been alive then — just to catch a glimpse of their long shaggy hair!

JEHESKEL SHOSHANI

The only other living elephant is the Asian (Elephas maximus). *This working individual, loading logs near Kandy in Sri Lanka, is a bull with well-developed tusks; female Asian elephants are often tuskless. The large unpigmented areas on its face are a feature of some Asian elephants. Although better known to many zoo-goers than its African cousin, the Asian is far rarer and has been fully protected from international trade for years.*

Once, prehistoric elephants and their kin — the mastodons, deinotheres and others — occupied environments ranging from desert to tropical rainforest and from sea level to high altitudes. With the exception of Antarctica, Australia, and some oceanic islands, the members of the order Proboscidea have at some time inhabited every continent on this planet. The most famous of them, the mammoths, were more closely related to the living Asian elephants than either is to the living African elephants. They looked more like Asian elephants, too, with their small ears and domed heads. I believe that there may once have been as many as 162 proboscidean species. Of these, 160 have become extinct.

All that remains of these great creatures are their skeletons, and, if we are lucky, a mummified carcass of a mammoth. Is this what we want for the Asian and African elephants — just skeletons and an occasional tuft of hair, a gallstone or mummified stomach contents? I know it is not what I want — certainly not after seeing Ahmed. It is the living creature, giving function to its strange form, that fascinates us.

Its form is certainly remarkable. For example, consider the trunk. This union of the nose and the upper lip is a highly sensitive and complex organ manipulated by over 100,000 muscle units. An elephant uses its trunk for feeding, watering, dusting, smelling, touching, sound production, lifting and as a weapon of defense and attack. What an indispensable, and yet unlikely, tool!

The tusks are another unlikely tool. An elephant's tusks are its second incisors, teeth that grow continuously at the rate of roughly seven inches (18 cm) per year. Early in development, each tusk bears a conical cap of smooth enamel which is worn off later. A mature tusk is composed mostly of dentine. Elephants may use their tusks to dig for water, salt and roots; to debark trees; as levers for maneuvering felled trees and branches; for display; for marking trees; as weapons; as trunk-rests; or as protection for the trunk (comparable to the bumper on a car). Just as humans are left- or right-handed, so too are elephants left- or right-tusked. The tusk that is used more than the other is called the master tusk and is shorter and more rounded at the tip because of wear.

Ivory has had some unexpected uses for human beings, too. Once it is removed from an elephant, ivory soon dries and begins to split unless it is kept cool and moist. Conversely, if it is kept in very hot and moist conditions, it will deteriorate. These water-absorbing properties of ivory are well known among certain African tribes, whose craftsmen and weathermen use ivory as a rain predictor by planting it in the ground in selected locations. High humidity would cause the ivory to swell, indicating the advent of rain.

Tusks are unusual enough, but even the elephant's cheek teeth grow strangely, sliding forward in the mouth as new ones develop from behind, as if they were on a conveyor belt. There is a reason for that, too. The cheek teeth are specially adapted to handle a highly abrasive diet of trees and plants—more than eighty different species in all. And, like everything else about it, an elephant's appetite is prodigious. A two- to seven-ton elephant requires about 160 to 330 pounds (75–150 kg) of food and about 20 to 45 gallons (80–160 L) of water per day. An extremely thirsty adult bull Asian elephant once drank 56 gallons (254 L) of water in less than five minutes. This massive intake of food and water means that an elephant must devote eighteen to twenty hours of its daily cycle to eating or searching for food or water.

Home ranges of elephants—the areas they wander in their search for all that food — vary in size from five to twenty square miles (15–50 km²) for cows and their offspring, and from two hundred to six hundred square miles (500–1,500 km²) for bulls. The differences depend on the quantity and quality of available food. This search for food and water sends elephants on long migrations. During the dry season, they gather in large concentrations near wetlands, where members of different families and herds intermingle. At the onset of the wet season, perhaps with the fall of the first raindrops, the appearance of the first dark clouds, or when the wind changes direction and velocity, queues of elephants begin to form. From a bird's-eye view, elephants within a basin several miles square seem to coordinate their movements and walk away from the center in all directions. Their paths lead towards savannahs and grasslands where they will spend most of the wet season. In the past, before the migration routes of many elephants were cut off by human settlement, a herd may have travelled from three thousand to six thousand miles (5,000–10,000 km) in a year to complete one cycle of seasonal migration. The amazing desert elephants of Namibia — animals weighing from two to seven tons, and requiring large amounts of food and water for their daily maintenance — trek a desolate landscape of barren land, rocks and sand dunes for sixty miles (100 km) or more a day.

Elephants travel along well-established paths that often follow a river basin, a valley, or a watershed. Human engineers have used these trails to establish the best possible baselines for roads along escarpments. One example is the old main road from Nairobi to Nakuru in Kenya, a highway that zigzags down to the Rift Valley floor overlooking a superb view of the volcanic mountains of Longanot and Suswa. The Italian prisoners of war

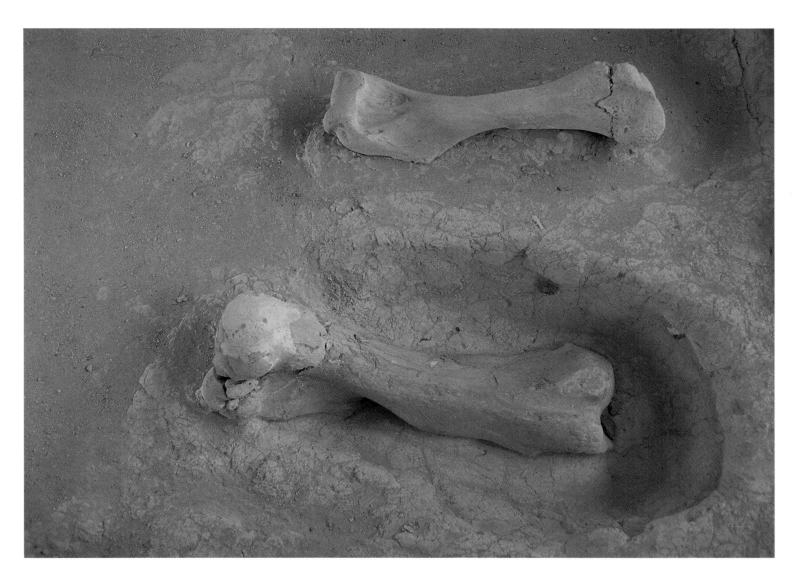

who built this highway during the First World War followed paths that were probably made by elephants.

The physical superlatives of elephants are matched by some of the most intricate and closely organized behavior patterns in nature. Elephants are highly social mammals, living in matriarchal family units composed of a cow and three to five of her immediate offspring. These units form the basic building block of a clan, or herd. The matriarch is usually the oldest in the group. Born and raised in her herd, she acquires her position through years of observing and learning from her older family members. Her leadership may be crucial during a drought, for example, when she must lead her family and relatives to the best possible foraging habitats.

Male elephants are usually driven away by older females when they reach puberty (at about thirteen years of age). They usually join or form bachelor herds, but may forage alone as Ahmed did for many years. Daughters, sisters and aunts, however, may remain with their families until death.

The key to their society is communication, whether it be by visual signs such as ear and trunk movements, by the release of odor-producing substances or by sounds. In fact, they use an extraordinary "secret" language. Elephants can produce low frequency sounds, which are not audible to the human ear but can travel long distances in the African savannahs

200,000-year-old humeri, or upper arm bones, of elephants unearthed by Louis and Mary Leakey at Olorgesaili, Kenya, a site that has also yielded tools of early man. The lower bone is from a young animal.

This bull in Chobe National Park, Botswana, is using his tusk as a trunk rest. A mature bull's trunk may weigh as much as 330 pounds (150 kg), a weight that needs to be redistributed occasionally to avoid straining his neck muscles. Notice the anal pad, a fat deposit at the base of the tail.

and grasslands and be heard by other elephants as much as a mile and a half (2.4 km) away.

It takes years for young elephants to learn the intricacies of their society. After a pregnancy of between eighteen and twenty-two months — the longest of any animal — newborn calves are tended by their mothers and by other females in the herd. It will be seven or eight years before the calf is completely weaned, and five years more before it has learned and matured enough to take its place as a breeding adult.

Elephants and man are more alike than we may realize. We share some of the longest life spans among mammals (elephants over 80 years, humans over 120 years), unspecialized food requirements, wide range of habitat occupancy, ability to modify our habitat, extended families, effective absence of predators on adults (if we exclude man), deferred sexual maturity, menopause or something like it, naked skin, cardiovascular diseases and arthritis, a long childhood associated with learning and tool use and manufacture. On one occasion an elephant, after digging a hole and drinking the water that seeped into it, stripped bark from a tree, chewed it into a large ball, plugged the hole and covered it with sand. Later he uncovered the sand, unplugged the hole and had water to drink.

In addition to ingenuity, elephants have, seemingly, displayed compassion and an awareness of death. There are stories of elephants using leaves and grass to bury elephant and human remains, and shattering the tusks of dead elephants against trees or rocks. Chandrasekharan, a trained Asian elephant, once refused to lower a pillar of wood into a hole. When his mahout approached the hole he found a dog sleeping at the bottom of the pit; only after the dog was chased away would the elephant complete his task. Is it any wonder we feel such a kinship with these astonishing animals?

Ever since the lineage of *Homo* in Africa evolved as a hunter-gatherer society, it appears to have been associated with the family Elephantidae. In many parts of the world mastodons, mammoths and elephants were

Hyraxes may not look much like elephants, but they are their closest living land relatives — as a Maasai legend suggests. Only the marine manatees and dugongs (Sirenia) are closer, and they don't look like elephants either. These three yellow-spotted rock hyraxes (Heterohyrax brucei) *were photographed at Lake Malawi, Malawi.*

exploited as a source of food, clothing and dwelling material. Archeologists have found remains of shelters built with elephant bones and tusks, as well as bones with butcher marks, charring and embedded projectile points. A half-million-year-old butchery site at Olduvai Gorge in Tanzania contained remains of the extinct elephant *Elephas reckii*, a cousin of the modern Asian elephant.

The first historical records of elephants — petroglyphs, pictographs, sculpture, figures on coins, and paintings — date back about five thousand years. Elephants have played important roles in Eastern religions. In Hinduism, the famous elephant deity Ganesh (or Ganesa) is considered the god of wisdom, good fortune and prudence. Although such strong religious connections between elephant and man did not evolve in Africa, hunters past and present, including illegal hunters such as poachers, revere elephants greatly. They may perform pre-hunt ceremonies and usually carry amulets made of elephant parts.

African and Eastern traditions were nurtured by many myths associated with elephants. The most remarkable one comes from the Maasai tribe of East Africa. When the god N'gai created the animals of the world, he made each in two forms, small and large. Thus, there were large pythons and small pythons, large storks and small storks, and large elephants and small elephants. The small elephants complained to their god that their trunks and tails were too long and got in the way when they were walking. N'gai was enraged. He reached into the jar of creation, cut their trunks and tails off and let them go among the rocks — and so were born the hyraxes. What is amazing about this legend is that hyraxes — animals that look like overgrown guinea pigs — really are the elephant's closest land relatives, a fact scientists did not discover until the turn of this century. Could the elders of the Maasai have realized this long ago?

Perhaps the most prevalent Western myth is the legend of the elephant graveyard, a secret place where elephants go to die. The idea of such a graveyard had its origin in the concentrations of elephant skeletons found close to marshy habitats where old elephants gather to eat the soft vegetation and many of them die. There are many other myths: elephants are afraid of mice (they are not); some have elephant bodyguards, as Ahmed was supposed to have; there are white elephants (albinos exist, but they are pinkish-gray); elephants have four knees (they have two knees and two wrists, like other mammals); and elephants have a passion for alcohol (some may deliberately eat overripe fruit). Elephant copulation has always piqued people's imagination. Some thought elephants conducted

A portrait of Ahmed, the elephant that inspired Jeheskel Shoshani to study elephants. His huge tusks may seem to be a burden even for so large an animal; in fact, they did not reach this size until Ahmed was well past breeding age and, for evolutionary purposes, no longer important as a producer of new elephants.

their amorous behavior in privacy, or copulated back to back. Others thought the male dug a hole for his mate so that they could mate easily. None of this is true; actually, elephants mate in the usual quadruped manner.

One widespread myth about the African elephant is that it cannot be domesticated. In fact, the first archeological evidence for domestication of African elephants comes from pictographs dating to the First Dynasty in Egypt, about 3200 B.C. In 218 B.C., during the Second Punic War, Hannibal, the Carthaginian general, crossed the Alps with thirty-seven elephants, apparently including Africans. The African elephants employed by Hannibal were probably North African. This population was depleted by extensive hunting long ago, and has left only silent witnesses of its existence in the form of petroglyphs and pictographs.

Relatively few people know of the African elephant training camp at Gangala-na-Bodio Station in Parc National de le Garamba, northeastern Zaire. This camp was the idea of King Leopold of Belgium in 1899. The camp has harnessed elephants to carts and plows, and has trained them as riding animals. The population of elephants at the station has fluctuated through the years; in 1982 there were eight elephants there, all female forest elephants.

In recent years the elephant has caught the world's attention, not as a source of fascination and folklore, or as man's helper, but as our defenseless victim. At the height of the ivory crisis at least seventy thousand elephants were being killed every year to supply the insatiable demand for "white gold." About 80 percent of the tusks came from poached, brutally killed elephants. Poachers indiscriminately shot males or females, young or old, many of whom were at prime reproductive age. As these operations continued, the average size of tusks taken grew smaller as adult males were eliminated and the poachers turned more and more to females and the young.

I have seen poachers in action and have had the opportunity to talk with them and with their captors. Some poachers are ruthless killers. Others kill elephants or rhinoceros not because they lack feelings for these animals, or because these animals play no part in their culture, legends or folklore. They poach because they are from low-income families and have been offered a handsome amount of money. Poaching is an opportunity they cannot refuse.

Poaching wildlife, elephants included, is part of a much bigger phenomenon—the human population explosion. Population pressure has certainly endangered the Asian elephant. Elephant poaching, on the other hand, has been almost nonexistent in Asia, partly because the tusks of the Asian elephant are small in males and normally absent in females. Yet in terms of numbers, the Asian elephant is in a far worse situation than its cousin in Africa. There are only a handful of them left in the wild. What is thirty to fifty thousand compared to the five to ten million which may have lived ten thousand years ago?

Some say that this is the way of the future—that as the human population grows, we must manage elephants like farm animals if they are to survive. These are certainly practical arguments. But for me, the awe and the love that elephants have inspired in me is enough to make me study them, try to understand them, and do what I can to save them in the wild.

It has been said that when a person observes elephants in the wild, that particular day, week, month or year is not counted in the person's life. My experience with Ahmed was the reason I came to spend so many days watching wild elephants in Africa and Asia; if the story is true, then Ahmed has extended my own life!

On January 17, 1974, Ahmed died, probably of natural causes. He was found the next day near Lake Paradise in the Marsabit Reserve. At his death he was about fifty-five years old, stood nearly ten feet (3 m) tall at the shoulder, and weighed about eleven thousand pounds (5,000 kg). Armed policemen and National Parks staff guarded his carcass during the four days it took to save his skin and transport it out of the Reserve to Nairobi, some three hundred miles (483 km) south. A fiberglass replica of his body now stands in the grounds of the National Museum of Kenya in Nairobi. Thousands of visitors from around the world view Ahmed's image and his mounted skeleton annually and record their memories on film and in notes. These are the witnesses for future generations.

Ahmed's fiberglass replica now stands outside the National Museums of Kenya in Nairobi. His skeleton is mounted indoors.

Will Ahmed's statue represent the last of his noble line? It is impossible to predict what will happen to the African elephant. Perhaps it will adapt. In some places elephants are already changing their habits, becoming shy during the day and active at night when they are safe. Instead of an Ahmed with ears spread wide, huge tusks and a trunk raised to trumpet, a different kind of elephant may develop: a stealthy, tuskless animal, which will communicate in a way that humans cannot hear, never announcing its presence. Perhaps it will be smaller and not require as much food. Perhaps it will move to remote areas and always be wary of its only natural enemy, ourselves.

There is an old Maasai saying: "You do not appreciate the value of something until you lose it." We have come close to losing the elephant. Can we not find ways to ensure that elephants like Ahmed, whether migrating across the Namib Desert or climbing through a closed canopy forest towards dark caves, will not vanish forever?

THE ELEPHANT HERD

The social system of African elephants is central to their life. Family groups of cows and their calves join together into bond-groups, bond-groups form clans, and clans may unite into herds of forty or more. The bonds between cows in the herd, particularly between close relatives, are very strong and may last a lifetime. The herds depend for their survival on the accumulated wisdom of their elders, and in particular on the matriarch who leads them. Bull calves are driven out of the herd at puberty, but often form small bachelor herds of from three or four to as many as ten animals.

Bull elephants normally do not associate with the herd. Like these three in the Zambesi Valley of Zimbabwe, they may form bachelor groups or forage alone.

The matriarch, leader of this herd in Botswana's Chobe National Park, threatens the photographer as the calves remain out of sight in the background, shielded by the other adults.

*Calm again, the herd moves
on, the cows, calves and
adolescents keeping close
together or even touching one
another with their trunks.*

Fresh from their mud wallow, a herd of cows and calves leaves a pan in Etosha Park, Namibia. The leg joint being flexed backwards by three of the animals is the wrist, not the knee. Confusion about this gave rise to the myth that elephants have extra knees.

The young elephant in this herd in Kenya's Amboseli National Park may seem too big to be still nursing, but calves are not fully weaned until they are seven or eight years old. His mother has large tusks and sunken temples, a sign of age; elephants as old as sixty-two years have been known to bear calves. The two medium-sized animals on the left are bulls, perhaps teenagers who will soon leave the herd.

Two bulls spar on the plains of Kenya's Amboseli National Park.

Following pages:
A herd of fifty or so elephant cows and calves, seen from the air in Zimbabwe's Hwange National Park, mills about in response to the airplane overhead.

A herd of cows and calves flees in alarm from a pan at Tsavo East National Park, Kenya, where heavy poaching has decimated the herds. The calves are kept in the center of the herd for protection, flanked by their older kin.

Two bulls walk through tall grass in the Zambesi Valley, Zimbabwe.

AN AFRICAN PERSPECTIVE

PEREZ OLINDO

I WAS BORN AND RAISED IN RURAL KENYA, UNDER THE TUTELAGE OF MY GRANDFATHER. He taught me about the motherhood of the land, and why the greatest care should be taken to safeguard its productive capacity. As for elephants, my introduction to them was through folklore. The giants that had once inhabited the land where we now lived had moved out generations earlier. What had once been prime elephant habitat was now crowded with human settlements, with their food crops and cash crops like tea and coffee. Even then, 120 years ago, the growth of the human population was the greatest threat to the survival of elephant herds in the wild.

My grandfather kept feeding me, night after night, on glowing accounts of the bravery of our ancestors, who had fought and conquered the lands that were now our tribal estate. He told me how elephants used to migrate through our land to unknown destinations, in search of salt and lush tall grasses that could only be found near the forests. Our people believed that the souls of our brave warriors reposed in elephants. For this reason, it was taboo for the Abaluhya people to hunt elephants or eat their meat. Even when it destroyed crops or caused a person's death, the worst that could happen to an elephant was that we would scare it away with drums or fire. Whenever our people came across ivory from dead elephants, it was entrusted to the tribal chief for ornaments. Ivory was never sold or given away.

That was at a time when barter was our only medium of exchange. Wealth was measured in terms of land area, in the number of cattle, sheep, goats and — in many African communities — the number of wives a man had. These reflected his status in the community Today, the influence of other cultures and the exposure of our people to a monetary economy have affected a shift in these basic, traditional beliefs. The old codes of conduct have, for many, changed.

My first direct encounter with elephants came years later. I saw my first elephant when I was seventeen years old, far away from my home district, while on a high-school expedition. Many emotions flowed

*Both the young female elephant and the giraffe (*Giraffa camelopardalis*) appear to be unconcerned by the other's presence in Etosha Park, Namibia.*

61

through me. I was amazed, I was excited, and I must admit that I was afraid, too. I immediately understood why such a majestic creature was treated with the reverence it received from our people. Little did I know, then, that I would later dedicate my entire working life to the conservation and active protection of these graceful animals and others; but this experience, and the lessons I had learned from my grandfather, led me to the study of zoology and wildlife management.

It was also my background that led me to resign from the Kenya Game Department in 1964, only nine months after joining government service. I resigned in protest at having been assigned the duties of "elephant control" — work which, in effect, involved shooting elephants considered to be in conflict with economic activities such as agriculture. Within me there was a strong feeling of moral objection to the instructions I had been given, instructions to kill animals that, for cultural, scientific and ethical reasons, I had held in the highest esteem all my life. I held, and still hold, the view that elephants and other animals have a right to life, and no human has any control over that right.

I then joined the National Parks of Kenya, and, ever since, my commitment has been to the protection of wild animals and their entire ecosystems. My association with wildlife has exalted my spirit, and imparted to me a respect for nature that no man-made institution can teach.

For the African people, the elephant has been a prominent part of their continent from time immemorial. Africans have either regarded elephants as a source of livelihood, or as the host of their ancestral spirits — which makes the elephant a sacred animal to such communities. Some African communities, greatly fearing for their safety and well-being, have migrated widely over the centuries to avoid elephants. Other, smaller groups of people started, in those early days, to kill elephants for commercial purposes. They have continued to do so in modern times. In the last fifty years or so, the species has been subjected to increasing hunting pressure, for no other reason than to acquire ivory for trade. This minority group of human destroyers has been largely responsible for the massive decline in the population of elephants across their entire range. My deep-seated fear is that unless humanity around the world stands together against this band of greedy, get-rich-quick people, the African elephant will become extinct, as did the dinosaurs — but for a more dishonorable reason.

We Africans have treated certain birds, animals and plants with the highest regard. In the cultural beliefs of some communities, the very existence of their lineage may depend upon a given wild species. Because these people are exceedingly grateful to the species concerned, other cultures have gone out of their way to describe them as "animists." In the English language, this description is neither fitting nor complimentary, and ignores the fact that so-called "animism" is really a moral principle whose observance has preserved Africa's wildlife heritage for generations. The future of living things is largely affected by the ethics of those who have influence over them.

Traditionally, Africans did not have the means or the need to kill animals for sport. They hunted only when they and other members of their community needed the meat for food, or the skins for domestic uses. Rarely did they leave usable parts to go to waste; and this remains true for the majority of those who still hunt today.

An elephant hunt was a momentous occasion. The planning of the hunt was detailed. The people who were selected to stalk, waylay or ambush the animals would rehearse their roles. Then special ceremonies, similar to praying for good omens and safety, would be undertaken. On the day of departure, entire communities would give the hunting party a warm send-off, in the full knowledge that not all those who were leaving for the hunt would live to return home. The hunted and the hunter had equal chances of survival. The humans seemed to have the better chance, because many of them converged on one selected animal and labored hard in their efforts to spear it to death. But because elephants have very strong family bonds, a hunted elephant always raised the alarm and attracted to its support the assistance of its family members. In this way, a fair duel was always fought between man and beast. If the elephants won the duel, many of the hunters lost their lives. If the people won, they had cause to celebrate. In this way, man lived in harmony, and on equal terms, with his environment. That is why we Africans consider modern hunting, with the human being mechanized and equipped with high-velocity firearms, as being equivalent to slaughter.

Many people I have encountered from the developed countries of the West have tended to credit themselves with teaching Africans to protect and conserve wildlife and their environment. No; the developed world taught Africans how to become efficient killers, using modern weapons. They taught Africans to kill wild animals for pleasure or, as it is called, sport. Africans have learned to kill and take away only trophies, leaving

A herd of mature elephant cows approaches through the brush of Samburu Reserve, one of the many national parks and reserves created by Kenya to protect its wildlife heritage.

63

the rest of the animal's biomass to go to waste. This kind of behavior is not typically African. Most older Africans would be horrified by it. They respect their environment and the animals that share it with them. These are the people who constitute the bridge between the generation gone by and those who now kill for commercial purposes. They represent a tradition that may become extinct like the elephant if both are not protected.

The poacher does not want the rest of his community to discover what he is doing, because he knows that his actions and intentions are against their common good. He moves in secret, to poach wildlife and to destroy the foundations of the environment and its resources. That is why the simple and honest celebrations of old do not accompany the evil deeds of the poachers. What is more, when the poacher returns from the hunt he shares nothing with his community. Rather, he is secretive and greedy, to the detriment of the species and the community.

By this time you may be wondering why I am dwelling on African hunting ethics when I am supposed to be writing about elephants. It is important that you understand that, to the African, these ethics are stronger than legislated public policy. For most of us, ethics are regarded as a way of life, and therefore part and parcel of the decision-making process. They have the force of religion. What I am saying in so many words is that if African hunting ethics had prevailed in decades past, the elephants — and many other animals, including the rhinos — would be in no danger of extinction today.

With the approach of independence, there was a widespread feeling that Africans should be brought rapidly into the business of wildlife conservation if the future of the National Parks and of wildlife in general was to be assured. Since I was the only African studying wildlife management at the time, I was asked to return home and start building bridges between the traditional African approach to wildlife management on the one hand, and the established institutions — national parks and the free range elsewhere in the country — on the other.

The task was not an easy one. The British who had administered Kenya had promoted big game hunting as a successful industry for themselves. Local communities were not allowed to take part. The resentment that this policy created meant that the British had no acceptable platform from which they could hand over the responsibility for the sustained management of the country's wildlife to the Africans.

When the colonial powers occupied Africa, they outlawed the ownership of guns by the native African peoples. They feared that if these communities were allowed to own arms, the colonizers' security would be threatened. The situation was further aggravated when laws were enacted restricting licenses for the hunting of wild animals to those people who owned, or possessed, the right caliber of firearms. Since hunting is inherent to African cultures, the people interpreted such prohibitions as having been designed to exclude them from their traditional hunting grounds, the lands that held the graves of their ancestors. They therefore retaliated against the foreign powers that had occupied their lands and now wanted to subjugate them.

The Africans militantly believed that all of the colonial legacy had to be destroyed and replaced by an image that was new and different. The planners of the emerging independent states wanted to develop and civilize Africa, and to enter into the modern, money-based global economy.

Their plans included clearing large stretches of land for cash crops. For the African masses, independence meant inheriting both political power and the land which, in Kenya, was the principal generator of wealth. However, there were not enough developed farms to go around. Those who could not inherit farms turned their attention to the forests. Others hatched similar designs for the national parks, which they conveniently saw as colonial relics. A number of such parks had been established by the colonial administration; they had been the preserves of foreigners, who had had the money to maintain them and use them as areas of recreation and relaxation.

The few political radicals who wanted to dismantle our national park system were not smart enough to realize that, after gaining independence, the rules of the game abruptly changed from destruction of the old system to the construction of a new sovereign state. Fortunately, a more enlightened group of freedom fighters prevailed, and Kenya has moved forward in her national development ever since.

My own objective, since then, has been to rekindle traditional African ethics regarding living in harmony with the environment. The single largest ongoing conservation activity in Kenya has been public awareness and conservation education. Our goal is to develop a constituency of indigenous, well-informed defenders of our wildlife. The success of that effort can be gauged by the nearly fivefold expansion of Kenya's National Parks only twenty-five years after independence.

But the legacy of the colonial restrictions still led some people to turn their weapons on the elephant as a gesture of defiance against the old regime. While this silent struggle between old and new attitudes towards the elephant was going on, markets for ivory were developing around the world. As the price of ivory increased, it gave these people an even better reason than simple resentment for killing elephants.

By this time, I had completed my studies and had worked my way up

The growth of Africa's population may be the greatest long-term threat facing African wildlife. Human settlements, like this one at Mbeya, Tanzania, cover much of what was once pristine elephant habitat.

the ladder to become the Director of one of the most prestigious national park systems in the world. Kenya was now a self-governing country, with Africans holding the reins of power. We soon discovered, however, that the respect for wildlife that had been part of our culture had, in many communities across the continent, been overshadowed by the power of money. I found myself training more and more rangers to try and contain the illegal slaughter that was being perpetrated by our own people.

From time to time I was drawn, even as Director, into active combat against poachers. To manage our greatly expanded national park system more efficiently, I had taken up flying. Although my primary objective in learning to pilot light aircraft had been to get to parks scattered across the country without wasting too much valuable time, during the late 1980s I found myself increasingly providing air cover to our ranger ground forces. I spent many hours each year following migrating herds of elephants, to ensure that they were safe from poachers who had become very efficient and highly mobile.

In 1988 three of my rangers were shot dead by poachers while they were on patrol. I was outraged, and I asked for increased government involvement in the battle to save the elephant. The president of Kenya, Daniel Arap Moi, announced his maximum support. Parliament debated the issue, and further funds were released to secure the safety of elephants; but the price of ivory continued to increase. Within weeks of the death of the three rangers, the aircraft I was piloting in support of an antipoaching operation came under automatic gunfire. Although the tip of one wing was hit, I and the other personnel who were travelling with me landed safely. Only two weeks later, three wildlife intelligence officers who had recovered several pairs of tusks and arrested the suspected poachers were stranded when their vehicle became stuck in the mud. The suspects raised the alarm, claiming that the officers were trying to kidnap them. Their fellow poachers came to their rescue, and killed the three officers. The driver escaped, with serious gun wounds, and was fortunately able to call for rescue on his walkie-talkie. He survived to tell the story.

When the government realized that the heavily armed men who were slaughtering the elephants and supplying the commercial ivory trade would not hesitate to kill anyone who opposed them, it adopted the policy of shooting poachers on sight. This was the only language these ruthless people could understand. Suffice it to say that the policy has been quite successful. The critics of our shoot-to-kill policy have always criticized the decision from the safety of their offices and homes. They have not realized that the effort to save elephants from extinction has turned into an open war for conservation.

Further, as a result of this policy, we have collected enough evidence to prove that this evil activity was being fuelled from outside Kenya. Soon after a peace treaty was signed between Ethiopia and Somalia, bands of heavily armed men moved into Kenya from the east, bringing automatic weapons. Although some Kenyans had taken to poaching, these outsiders were the people who almost eradicated Kenya's elephant population.

What happened in Kenya could happen elsewhere. Since the struggles leading to independence in most African countries, military and economic instability have gripped Africa. Firearms have proliferated throughout the continent. Hungry and impoverished people, who also happen to be heavily armed, find it difficult to resist turning those arms against innocent animals. We fear that as peace returns to Namibia, Angola and Mozambique, the scenario of eastern Africa could repeat itself. I do not want to be misunderstood. My hope is that the countries in the southern parts of Africa can contemplate our experience, and prepare to manage crises of a similar type and possibly of the same magnitude.

Now that international commercial trade in ivory has been banned and the ivory market has collapsed, the time has come to ponder the future of the African elephant. We must find a lasting solution for its survival — one that will provide answers for the countries that have the responsibility of looking after elephants. Surely that solution must have its roots in the cultures of the African people, and must be linked to their aspirations for economic development. Ways must be found for living elephants to generate both employment and wealth for the communities that live and share their environment with them. We must find a way for elephants and man to coexist.

We know that it is not cheap to protect one elephant; it is that much more expensive to guarantee the security of thousands. Elephants need very large areas to supply the food and minerals necessary for their survival. By setting aside national parks for them, the countries that are promoting elephant conservation are doing so by sacrificing other economic activities that could be generating real wealth for their peoples. They — and particularly the local communities that are immediately affected — are therefore justified in demanding specific economic returns for sharing their lands with elephants and other wildlife.

For some of the countries of Africa, such as Kenya, a part of this solution lies in "ecotourism." Ecotourism must be organized so that the local communities that participate in the protection and conservation of the elephant receive economic returns from the tourist industry. This approach is not theoretical; it has been adopted in some parts of Kenya, and the results are very encouraging. Wherever the people have been

This elephant-crossing sign in Hwange National Park, Zimbabwe, demonstrates one of the ways that man must make room for the elephant if both are to coexist in Africa.

67

given an economic interest in wildlife — or in any other resource — they have regarded it as an asset and therefore worth saving.

The Kenyan approach is only one way of planning for the future security of elephants. In other parts of Africa, communities for whom elephants are an important source of food are making sustainable proposals to harvest a limited number of elephants for their use. In return they will guarantee the security of the remaining, and — we hope — increasing, elephant herds.

Those of us who have been directly connected with the conservation of elephants know how difficult it is for the African countries to protect these great mammals on their own. We call for nothing less than a global plan of action, with external funding for elephant conservation.

Remember that poaching is but one of the threats the elephant faces. Where human land use has transformed the ecosystem, elephants have moved away to safer localities. Accordingly, the rapidly increasing human population in Africa does not augur well for the future security of elephants or of other large, gregarious mammals. Other, newer threats are desertification and global warming. Harsh desert conditions do not allow the prolific growth of the grass and browse elephants need. Desertification and excessive hunting have totally eliminated elephants in the Sahara and most of the upper Sahel zone. Some readers may dismiss global warming as a hoax, but we who are managing the natural ecosystems have observed a 10 percent drop in soil moisture content. Grasses and shrubs whose minimum water requirements are not met will simply perish, making the ecosystem less and less accommodating for large-scale eaters like the elephant. These issues must — and are — being addressed on a global scale.

The challenge is tremendous. In most of the countries of West Africa, only remnant populations of elephants remain. It will require an extraordinary degree of commitment if they are to recover to viable numbers. Large-scale poaching in East Africa has almost certainly set the course towards the fragmentation of elephant populations and the disruption of family groups and social structure in a manner similar to what now exist in West Africa. It is in anticipation of the promise of recovery in West and East Africa that the international community must be asked to guarantee that rampant and illegal trade in ivory never begins again.

There has always been controversy as to whether the ivory trade should continue in some form. Ivory is largely ornamental; it is not essential for human survival. Obtaining it, however, costs the lives of elephants and of human beings. Those who intend to buy it should make sure that they have seen a living elephant first, in a zoo or in the wild, before making that conscious decision that one of these giants must die to make it possible for them to enhance their own personal beauty.

My grandfather taught me to revere the animals around me as living creatures, with their own right to a place in our land. Today, in my work for the African Wildlife Foundation, I am trying to spread that message around the world on behalf of elephants and other creatures. In doing so I believe that I am spreading the virtues of my own African heritage, the legacy that my grandfather bequeathed to me. I believe that this heritage of respect for the animals around us is what we need if we are really to save the African elephant.

Two three- to four-year-old calves, orphaned by culling operations in Zimbabwe, receive a reassuring touch from their human keeper in their new home at Mukuvisi Woodlands on the outskirts of Harare.

YOUNG ELEPHANTS

Only man, among mammals, has a longer childhood than the elephants.
African elephant babies may nurse for seven or eight years, and reach
puberty at about the same age as humans. During their long calfhood
they learn the behaviors of elephant society, and at about ten they begin
to take on some of the duties of caring for their younger siblings.
Tragically, the slaughter of elephants has left a growing number of
orphans—sometimes, in East Africa, whole herds of them. Some lucky
ones may find themselves with human foster-parents at Daphne
Sheldrick's orphanage in Kenya, or at Mukuvisi Woodlands in Zimbabwe,
where a few young survivors of culling operations have been reared
under the auspices of the Zimbabwe Wildlife Society.

*Two calves head off down a
trail at Mukuvisi Woodlands,
Zimbabwe.*

A cow in Namibia's Etosha Park tends her two calves. The younger is about a year old, the older perhaps five; the calving interval for elephants is roughly four years. Both are still of nursing age. In two or three years the older calf will be fully weaned, and by the age of ten will be able to help care for its younger siblings.

A yearling calf dogs its mother's dusty footsteps in Namibia's Etosha Park. A quick rule of thumb for guessing a calf's age: if it is short enough to pass under its mother's belly, it is probably under a year old. The cow clearly shows the almost triangular forehead of female African elephants; bulls have a more rounded profile.

Two adolescent bulls, their
childhood in the herd nearly
over, spar in Botswana's
Chobe National Park. One
is discharging a secretion
from his temporal gland.
They butt each other with the
thick-skinned bases of their
trunks, the thin-skinned tips
safely tucked out of the way.

A cow shades her sleeping calf from the sun in Etosha Park, Namibia. Jeheskel Shoshani has watched cow elephants at Etosha shift their position as the sun crossed the sky, always making sure that their shadows fell on their calves. Notice that even in sleep the calf stays in physical contact with its mother. The antelope in the background is a greater kudu (Tragelaphus strepsiceros).

A cow and her calf threaten the photographer on a dusty road in the Chobe National Park, Botswana. Even very young calves will spread their ears in imitation of their parents.

A road in Kenya's Maasai Mara National Park cuts through the home range of this yearling calf.

These two calves at Mukuvisi Woodlands, Zimbabwe, appear to be about two years old; they have already lost their milk tusks, but the adult tusks have yet to emerge.

Two orphaned calves, about two years old, at Mukuvisi Woodlands, Zimbabwe, pause for a drink.

Preceding pages:
Rump to trunk, a teenager and a calf stride across a plain in Chobe National Park, Botswana. Calves are often tended by their older sisters, and that may be the case here. Elephants of all ages appear to derive some comfort from physical contact.

Alarmed, a calf at Mukuvisi Woodlands, Zimbabwe, spreads its ears, raises its foot and turns the tip of its trunk backwards to catch the scent of the photographer.

81

82

WHEN THE FOREST FALLS SILENT

DAVID WESTERN

IT'S CLEAR THAT OUR WORLD IS GREENING. NO POLITICIAN TODAY CAN IGNORE THE groundswell. We recognize the vulnerability of our tremendous biological wealth inherited from eons of evolution, the possibility of an extinction spasm that could see one quarter of all earth's species exterminated by the end of this century, and the grave risks indeed to our own welfare. We have come to accept our custodianship of nature, to allow that wilderness is the one frontier we can hand on, unconquered, mysterious and exciting, to future generations. We have moved on to the notion that conservation is possible if we include it with the notion of sustainable development, and this has become our own modern mantra.

E. O. Wilson of Harvard University, author of *Sociobiology*, says it best: "The worst thing that can happen is not energy depletion, economic collapse, limited nuclear war or conquest by a totalitarian government. These catastrophes can be repaired within a few generations. The one process that will take millions of years to correct is the loss of genetic and species diversity by the destruction of natural habitats. This is a folly our descendants are least likely to forgive us."

The threats are plain enough. Most of our biological wealth resides in the tropics, half of it in the tropical forests. Yet an area the size of Costa Rica is burned, logged and converted to farms every year. The forest could be gone, and its diversity lost, within a mere thirty years.

We generally recognize that the greatest threat is habitat loss and fragmentation, and the most immediate solution is the creation of protected areas. Throughout my professional career I have championed the idea of conservation of ecosystems through the participation of indigenous and local peoples. But more recently I have come to realize that by ignoring the threats to certain species, we are in danger of saving nature's estate and losing its tenants. We may end up saving large tracts of land as biologically bleak as the American prairies after the extermination of the bison.

We have never learned to temper our demands, to use the fruits of the natural world sustainably. The quagga, bison, whale and the world's

The rainforests of Central Africa, home of the forest elephant (Loxodonta africana cyclotis), *are falling to the axe—as are rainforests the world over. This photograph was taken in the Congo.*

83

tropical forests are proof enough of this. The specter of Pleistocene over-kill—the disappearance roughly ten thousand years ago of one half of the world's large mammals, possibly at the hands of early man—still haunts us.

Most of us do not recognize the benefits of cooperating with nature, or realize its relevance. What does the loss of thousands of unnamed and little-loved insects mean to the average Tanzanian? What he needs is something visible and relevant—something his children will talk about, like the Indian his tiger, and the Californian his condor.

No species underscores the point better than the African elephant. We must look back two decades to understand the elephant crisis. We owe a great deal to Iain Douglas-Hamilton, who undertook the first pan-African surveys of elephants on behalf of the African Elephant Specialist Group of the International Union for the Conservation of Nature (IUCN). He tried to find out how many there were, where they were, and the status of the species. He concluded in his final report, produced in 1979, that elephants were in rapid decline due to the ivory trade. Full of confidence, he invited Ian Parker, a wildlife manager, ex-warden and specialist on the trade, to undertake a major investigation of the ivory trade under a contract from the U.S. Fish and Wildlife Service.

Parker arrived at diametrically opposed conclusions. He found that the elephant was not in trouble, and that its numbers were perhaps as many as three million, most of them hidden in the Central African forest. He also concluded that the ivory trade could be supported by natural mortality alone—that is, by collecting the tusks from elephants that had died from natural causes.

The difference between the two studies, and the lack of hard data, left the conservation world in confusion. After a contentious meeting of IUCN's African Elephant Specialist Group, held in Wankie, Zimbabwe, in 1981, there was still no satisfactory plan for the African elephant.

Shortly afterwards, as Chairman of the African Elephant and Rhino Specialist Group (AERSG), I was asked to resolve the standoff. One thing was immediately clear: elephants needed more concerted efforts to resolve their status. They deserved the best.

Over the next three years I assembled an impressive number of experts to look at all aspects of the ivory trade and elephant conservation. Iain Douglas-Hamilton resumed his counts and came up with better population estimates. Richard Barnes of Wildlife Conservation International undertook the most comprehensive wildlife surveys ever done in the 800,000 square miles (2,000,000 km²) of uncharted tropical forest in Central Africa. Finally, Tom Pilgram, a Berkeley anthropologist, and I investigated the elephant's status, using mathematical population models. By 1987 the results were in. At a meeting held in Nyeri, Kenya, the AERSG stated very clearly that the elephant was in decline, largely because of the ivory trade.

How were we to respond? We still knew far too little about the ivory trade and about poaching in Africa. Although rhinos were being poached to near-extinction, a trade ban had made no difference whatsoever to their status. An ivory trade ban was equally unlikely to work without knowing how the trade worked, and without wide support both in Africa and in the consumer nations. I therefore initiated the most comprehensive study yet of the African elephant, in which thirty-five specialists, forming the Ivory Trade Review Group (ITRG), looked in detail at the ivory trade.

The results of this study, convened in July 1988 and completed in May 1989, were compelling. Between 1970 and 1989 Kenya's elephant population had declined from 140,000 to less than 17,000, Tanzania's from 200,000 to a little over 65,000, and Uganda's from 18,000 to a few hundred. The pattern was similar in Central Africa. One or two populations — in northern Congo and Gabon — were secure. The rest were in rapid decline. The only exception was in southern Africa, where some 150,000 elephants were still safe in Botswana, Zimbabwe and South Africa.

Overall, elephant populations were halving every ten years. That rate of decline was ten times faster than the rate of elephant habitat loss through agricultural expansion, and five times greater than human population increase. Most of the elephants were being lost inside national parks and deep forests, where the pressure of human population is not great. Poaching for ivory was indisputably the main reason for this decline, dwarfing all others. We knew that without a letup in the trade, that loss would accelerate in the coming years.

What about the global pattern of the trade? In recent years most ivory had been exported by Sudan, the Central African Republic, the Congo and Zaire. This volume of exports had nothing to do with the number of elephants in those countries; laundering had obscured the ivory's true origin. Burundi, which boasted one elephant up until 1987, was once the major exporter of ivory for the whole of Africa. It became the conduit for illegal ivory throughout the entire continent.

Most exports were bound for the Far East — Hong Kong, Singapore and Japan. Hong Kong was the major entrepôt, where ivory was carved and reexported to other countries, particularly Japan, Europe and America. Japan consumed 40 percent of the world's ivory, and Europe and America took about a third. As elephant numbers, and exports, declined, these hard-currency countries drove up the price of ivory in bidding wars.

This cow elephant and her calf, who is probably about two years old, are feeding in a grassy swamp in Kenya's Amboseli National Park. By trampling and eating the tall vegetation that surrounds them, elephants make such swamps available to many of Amboseli's smaller animals.

Following pages:
Plains animals like these zebras (Equus burchelli) *in Ngorongoro Crater, Tanzania, can be driven out of an area by bush encroachment. By clearing undergrowth, elephants make it possible for zebras to live in areas that would otherwise be closed to them.*

The total export value from Africa of ivory was worth on the order of $50 to $60 million a year, but only a tiny portion of that, some $5 to $6 million, went back into Africa. Most of it ended up in foreign bank accounts. Our ivory trade study had dispelled one major illusion: the ivory trade, which was worth $1 billion worldwide, was worth virtually nothing in Africa.

What was the impact of the trade on elephant populations? Two independent studies gave similar results. First, Graeme Caughley of the Australian Commonwealth Scientific and Industrial Resources Organization (CSIRO) predicted that elephants would become extinct throughout Africa by the year 2010, and in East Africa within five to seven years, unless the trade slackened. Caughley's report was a bombshell. Although commissioned by the CITES Secretariat, it never saw the light of day. It was therefore all the more important that the Ivory Trade Review Group, which I had commissioned to prepare an open study, did not suffer the same fate. Our results were remarkably similar to Caughley's, though our assumptions were more conservative. We concluded that the African elephant would be extinct within the next twenty-five to thirty years at the present level of trade.

In an earlier study, Tom Pilgram and I had made a startling discovery: we did not need to kill elephants to have a sustainable ivory trade. If we wanted to manage ivory most profitably and sustainably, we were going about it the wrong way. We should allow elephants to age and die naturally. This natural mortality would yield four times more ivory than would poaching. The reason for this is that elephants add most of the ivory to their tusks late in life. In addition, big pieces of ivory are worth more per kilo than small ones. The result is that very big elephants give the highest yield economically.

Over the last thirty years the big tuskers have disappeared from Africa. Between 1965 and 1969, 81 percent of all the ivory leaving Africa came from elephants having tusks over twenty-two pounds (10 kg). Between 1979 and 1984, only 13 percent had tusks that large. In other words, the big tuskers had long since vanished, and in their place small bulls were being shot. The average age of bulls now being shot for tusks is twelve years, that is, barely at the age of puberty.

The picture is very similar for female elephants. Adult females — the big matriarchs — are very important to the herds. They lead them on their migrations and have the wisdom to know how to avoid threats, including poaching. These, too, had been killed. Over 55 percent of all the elephants killed for the trade in the late 1980s were reproductive females, and most of the remainder were juveniles and infants. While ten years ago only a small proportion of all elephants that died due to the ivory trade were the orphans of poached mothers, that figure has now risen to a quarter of all deaths.

According to Joyce Poole, now Elephant Program Coordinator for the Kenya Wildlife Service, the fragmentation of the herds has led to a loss of the knowledge elephants need for migration, foraging and social bonding. The loss of bulls and healthy females may be lowering the reproductive rate, though we have no proof of that yet.

All these compelling arguments and statistics make a powerful case for curbing the ivory trade — but they are not enough. They hinge on the premise that elephants are valuable only for ivory. I contend that we must consider the broader value of elephants, in particular their remarkable role as a key species in Africa's forests and savannahs. We must see the threat to the elephant as a threat to an entire ecological system.

Overgrazing by livestock causes bush encroachment over much of Africa. Bush then becomes infested by the tsetse fly, which is inimical to human populations and livestock alike. In the past, elephants thinned dense bush, reduced the tsetse fly population, increased grasslands, and thus increased the opportunity for livestock use in an area. Today, they play a similar role outside national parks, counteracting the effects of the overgrazing that is common on commercial ranches.

But there's a far more fascinating story to be told. Elephants are responsible in part for maintaining the diversity, the biodiversity in modern parlance, of Africa's forests and savannahs. They are responsible for the zebra and wildebeest being there. They do this by acting as an ecological bulldozer. By opening up dense habitats and maintaining a state of ecological flux, they diversify the plant and animal community, creating space for a variety of species.

For the last twenty years I have worked in Amboseli National Park in southern Kenya. Amboseli is one of the few places in Kenya where elephants have been reasonably safe from poachers. Twelve years ago we introduced a policy of benefiting local landowners through revenues from the national park. Since these landowners are now receiving direct revenues, they regard the wildlife as their own animals. The Maasai have long had a tradition of regarding wildlife as what they call their second cattle. They say, "We milk cattle. We get money from them." They recognize that any poacher who kills a rhino or an elephant is eliminating one of the most important attractions of Amboseli, so they have been active in informing the wildlife department when poachers come into the area. As a result, Amboseli's elephants have increased.

At Amboseli I have been able to watch the progress of a natural experiment. Outside the park, where poaching has removed elephants, the woodlands have become dominated by a single species. They have become so dense that in the understory there are virtually no other plants.

The Maasai, unlike many Western cattle owners, understand the need to share their grazing lands with wildlife. In Tanzania's Ngorongoro Conservation Area, wildlife, the Maasai and their cattle coexist, as here in the famous Ngorongoro Crater.

Kenya's Amboseli National Park is one of the few places in East Africa where elephants have been reasonably safe from poachers. Adults with tusks this large have been exterminated almost everywhere else.

In the park, elephants have opened up these thickets, creating a patchwork of woodlands and grasslands that supports both grazing and browsing animals. Some areas I studied once supported only elephant and rhino. Today I can see wildebeest and zebra in areas that only ten years ago were too thick to be available to these grassland species. In the park's woodlands I can still find a variety of bush species such as impala, Grant's gazelle, gerenuk, and giraffe.

Amboseli's swamps also benefit from elephant activities. Swamps are important late-season reserves for wildlife, particularly the grazing animals. In 1971, tall sedges, too coarse for zebra, wildebeest and gazelle to feed upon, grew densely around the swamp outside my house in Amboseli. Elephants, however, trampled and ate the sedges during droughts, to the point where smaller animals could survive on the regenerating reeds. As elephants increased in Amboseli, they opened up its swamps and made them available to many other species that could not have otherwise used them. Today, the same area has a mixture of species — buffalo, zebra, wildebeest and gazelle.

The picture is really no different in the vast forests of Central Africa. We are only beginning to realize how crucial the elephant is to the architecture and the dynamics of Africa's forests.

The typical forest elephant (*Loxodonta africana cyclotis*), with its sloped-back head, very long tusks, short ears, straight back and truncated rear end is a rather different creature from the familiar animals of the savannah (*Loxodonta africana africana*). We know so little about the forest that it wasn't until 1986, when I went on a trip with Richard Barnes and author Peter Mattheissen, that we finally resolved the mystery of the "pygmy elephant," an animal some insisted was a separate species. We saw so-called "pygmy elephants." They were undersized animals with well-developed tusks. They looked like full-grown bulls simply because their tusks were so advanced, but, in fact, they were very young males, probably no more than about eight to nine years old. The forest elephant, it turns out, has an extraordinarily precocious tusk development. Its tusks grow extremely quickly, so that by the time it is four years old, it looks like an elephant that, in the savannahs, I would have considered to be ten to fifteen years of age.

That solved part of the mystery, but there is another side of this story that is equally intriguing. We discovered that there are actually two elephants in the forest, as the pygmy has always claimed — and as the naturalists, including myself, have thoroughly misunderstood. The big one is the bush elephant, the same animal that lives on the savannahs. What we didn't realize is that it also occurs throughout the forest, alongside the typical forest elephant. Perhaps the flux of the forest back and forth across Africa has been so volatile, so quick — geologically speaking — that the forest and the savannah elephant became locked together in one habitat for several thousand years, during which time they began to hybridize.

A tropical forest looks extraordinarily lush, but in fact it produces little more vegetative material than a moist savannah. Most of its new growth is either inert wood that herbivores cannot eat, or is produced high in the canopy ceiling, where ground-dwelling animals cannot reach it. For all the greenery overhead, the forest floor is a remarkably sterile place. I have seen this in the forests of the Central African Republic. Very little light penetrates to the ground beneath the immense height of the

When large numbers of elephants become confined to isolated, protected areas and are unable to migrate, they can devastate their habitat. This mopane woodland in Hwange National Park, Zimbabwe, shows the result: trampled undergrowth, dead and dying trees. In Zimbabwe, the solution to overcrowding is to cull the herds; Kenya, among others, is experimenting with less drastic approaches.

trees — 150 feet (46 m) or more. The understory is a very inimical place, particularly to the larger plant-eaters that live there.

We are beginning to realize that it is the continual dynamism of the forest, the continual changes, that are the secret of its diversity. And if there is any one creature — other than man — that creates that degree of change it is the elephant. Elephants eat young seedlings, break down saplings and keep the forest glades open so that understory plants can grow. By doing this, they bring the primary production — the edible plant growth of the forest — down from the ceiling to the floor, and make it available to many other creatures, such as buffalo, duiker, okapi, bongo, sitatunga, giant forest hog and many other species. The abundance of these species, and the diversity of the forest, depends on the role the elephant plays as the forest's grand architect. When the elephant disappears, the forest falls silent.

There is an ironic flip side to the story. The loss of elephants threatens biodiversity, yet too many elephants can produce the same problem. Poaching forces elephants to flee to safe areas, especially national parks like Amboseli. I have seen what overcrowded elephants can do to a park. They smash up areas of woodland to such an extreme that there are very few plants left. The shattered trees then become vulnerable to fires, which eliminate most of the remaining woody plants.

The situation is probably no different in the forests. In Garamba National Park in Zaire, elephant overcongestion has reduced areas that were once forest to mere remnants. So the forests have fallen silent there, but for quite another reason. By compressing elephant populations into a few safe areas, we have become victims of our initial success in protecting the elephant.

Poaching has created two polar opposites: the loss of elephants outside national parks, and the compression of elephants inside national parks. Both are prejudicial to biodiversity. That seemingly innocent bracelet bought at Tiffany's is impoverishing Africa's forests and savannahs.

What could this mean for Africa? We have to go to Costa Rica in tropical Central America to understand the implications. There, Dan Janzen, Professor of Biology at the University of Pennsylvania, has become well known in his efforts to try and reconstruct dry forests. He has realized that it is the loss of the Pleistocene megafauna — the giant animals that lived there ten to fifteen thousand years ago — that has resulted in the

IAN REDMOND

A zone of densely growing bamboo extends from 7,500 feet (2 286 m) to between 8,500 feet (2 590 m) and 9,800 feet (2 987 m) in the mountain forests of the Virunga Volcanoes of Rwanda and Zaire. Here the few remaining forest elephants of the Virungas must force broad pathways to reach the Hagenia *woodlands higher up—as must human beings if they are to reach the home of the mountain gorilla.*

impoverishment of so much of Central America's forests. Trees like the guanacaste have big seeds that were once dispersed by the gomphothere, an extinct relative of the elephant, and other large mammals. Today they have no seed dispersers. Those important large plants have therefore been reduced to a few areas. The forests have become simplified.

There is more at stake, then, than the extinction of the elephant. Its loss will create a domino effect; we are liable to lose many other species in the process. South African ecologist Norman Owen-Smith has shown that the loss of elephants in Natal's Hluhluwe Reserve in the last century led to intense bush encroachment and the extinction of grazing species within the sanctuary. That process will be repeated over most of Africa if we exterminate elephants outside parks and overcrowd them within.

The debate over the ivory trade has ignored the broader economic as well as ecological value of elephants. One example of this non-ivory value makes the point admirably. A study recently undertaken in Kenya by Gardner Brown of the University of Washington looked at how much money people spend, directly and indirectly, on elephants. He concluded that over $20 million can be attributed solely to elephant viewing. Furthermore, if elephant numbers were halved from Kenya's present twenty thousand, the tourist trade would likely suffer an $80-million-dollar loss. In Kenya alone, the indirect value of elephants exceeds the notional value of the ivory trade — that is, the value it would have in a legal market — tenfold, and the value to Africa as a whole some fourfold.

There is yet another way in which the elephant is important economically — a view advanced in Southern Africa. Here overcrowded elephants inside national parks, as in East Africa, are reducing biological diversity. Zimbabwe and South Africa protect their biological diversity by culling elephants. Money from meat and sport hunting is ploughed back to local peoples through the Campfire Programs, and fosters their involvement in the process.

The elephant has become a home-grown symbol on a continent where extinction is a stranger — the quagga and the bluebuck in southern Africa being exceptions. Extinction, to the average African, is meaningless: our species are as old as our myths and legends. The threat to the elephant has finally brought the message home: the elephant is Africa's California condor, its tiger, its panda. If we lose our elephants and rhinos, we condone an avalanche of extinctions.

The reason we have undervalued the elephant has been our penchant for a single product — ivory. With its value so high, we had no hope of protecting elephants from poachers on our poor continent. It takes more than $1,000 per square mile ($400 per square kilometer) to protect the elephant in southern Africa. The elephant had become a walking gold mine, which cost more to protect than we could earn from ivory. No number of lives lost in protecting the elephant would save it. The rhino, whose horn is worth more than its weight in gold, has demonstrated that message most tragically.

What were the options? The Ivory Trade Review Group (ITRG) first looked at ways to use ivory and other elephant products sustainably. The reality was that elephants, like the great whales, are already so heavily overhunted that it will take years for their numbers to recover. The ivory trade was already in steep decline; the carvers would be out of work one way or another. Only by halting the ivory trade immediately would there be any options for the future. The priorities for elephant conservation should be based not on ivory, but on the other values elephants provide for Africa.

ITRG recommended placing the elephant on Appendix I of CITES because it was imminently endangered, with certain exceptions in southern Africa. We recognized that prices would skyrocket during the ninety days before the ban became effective. To forestall a poaching spree and prevent the market from going underground, ITRG recommended immediate import bans in all consumer countries. The outcome, coming at a time when the international press was championing the cause of elephants, was almost inevitable.

The collaborative efforts of many organizations, including Wildlife Conservation International, the World Wildlife Fund, and IUCN, precipitated the bans in the United States, Europe, Hong Kong, Japan and Dubai in June and July of 1989. The domestic bans foreshadowed the outcome of the CITES meeting in October, and gave an early indication of how effective an international moratorium might be. However, the import bans created a furor among the African countries when they met in Botswana that July.

The southern African countries, with good reason, argued that their elephants were safe. The issue, to the rest of Africa, was not so much their protective measures as the large volume of illegal ivory flowing through southern Africa. Unless the South came up with fail-safe ways to stop the laundering of ivory, elephants would still be endangered.

The gulf between African countries remained unbridgeable at the CITES conference. A straight Appendix I (endangered species) listing failed. The compromise was a modified Appendix I. In recognition of the likelihood that the southern African countries would trade outside the legal instrument of CITES, special provisions were made to downlist safe populations—providing the trading system proved no threat to other populations.

In the three months after the domestic bans came into effect, the price of ivory in Zaire dropped 50 percent, and the price of ivory in Hong Kong dropped 30 percent. The big stockpiles in Burundi and Hong Kong were virtually unmoveable. The surfeit of ivory on the world market increased further after the CITES ban, and poaching has dropped over most of Africa —a truly remarkable turnaround. I firmly believe that if the United States, Europe and Japan stand firm, the elephant is likely to be safe from the poachers' depredations. After all, there are still 600,000 elephants in Africa — enough to ensure that they can reestablish their vital ecological role, rather than just survive in a few sanctuaries like the black rhino.

What is the future of the African elephant? Many African countries have taken the elephant as a symbol, and perhaps none more poignantly than Kenya, where President Moi burned over twelve tons of ivory and appealed for an international ban. I see this as a symbolic victory, but only as a symbolic victory. It could be a turning point, or only a media flash in the pan—one of those fifteen-second sound bites the public thrives on.

It will take more than an ivory ban, however, to save the elephant in the long term. Overutilization is universal, whether of flounder off the coast of the United States and Canada or of pandas in China. The laws of supply and demand work poorly for commercially valuable, free-ranging species. Overharvesting is worst with slow-growing species, such as elephants. Harvests of 5 percent a year, about as much as elephants can sus-

Tourists and elephants can meet at extremely close quarters. This bull grazing next to a camper's tent was photographed at Mana Pools National Park in Zimbabwe. Unlike some African national parks, Mana Pools has no lodges, and camping provides the only means to stay there.

tain, are paltry compared to the value of killing all the elephants, selling off their ivory and investing in high-rises in Hong Kong at a 15 percent rate of return.

The problem lies with our value system. We tend to treat nature like a bottomless cookie jar. Fortunately, our attitude is changing. We are becoming aware of the planet as Spaceship Earth. We are beginning to realize our dependence on nature—that our futures are intimately bound. More recently, we have been willing to forgo profit in the interest of protecting species, no less than works of art in museums. If we are willing to preserve art, why not nature? Why not the elephant?

That answer, though honorable, is not good enough for third world countries battling for survival. Trying to convince the farmer in Africa that the elephant munching his crops has any possible value is quite a different issue. The challenge is to spare the agony of the African farmer who confronts the elephant day to day. The elephant must have practical, tangible meaning to the life of the average African, whether it is through tourism, as in Kenya, or through utilization, as in the Campfire Programs of Southern Africa. If we can make the elephant and other species of value in Africa, they will survive until we can afford to value them for their own sake.

The Year of the Rhino, the Year of the Whale, the Year of the Rainforest—they are all behind us. Yet the problems of extinction and degradation are still with us. Let me finish with the words of Russ Train, President of the World Wildlife Fund: "The whales, the rhinos, the tigers, the elephants—these are the visible tip of the iceberg. What we are really talking about is the biological impoverishment of the planet." The elephant is more than a single species. It is a symbol, an ecological keystone. Valuing it in that way we can save the elephant, the savannahs and the forests.

A CITES ban has been powerless to stop the poaching of the black rhinoceros (Diceros bicornis), whose horn is demanded by Yemenis for ceremonial dagger handles and by many people in the Orient for its fictitious medicinal properties. Over 95 percent of the rhino population has been slaughtered in the past two decades. Many opponents of the ivory ban predicted a similar failure for the elephant.

95

THE DIVERSITY OF LIFE

The richness of Africa's wildlife is proverbial. We now know that much of that richness depends on the African elephant. At normal population densities, elephant activities create habitat for many other species of animals. Because elephants require so much territory, when we save elephants in the wild we save a host of smaller creatures; land that can support one elephant will support four bushbucks, or nineteen hyraxes, or any number of birds, reptiles, frogs and insects. If humankind can make Africa safe for elephants, the survival of many of the creatures in this photo essay — and a myriad more — should be assured.

A lone Burchell's zebra foal (Equus burchelli) *stands on a hilltop at Maralal, Kenya. Animals of the open plains, zebras benefit greatly from the bush-clearing activities of elephants.*

A lioness (Panthera leo) *rests in the woodlands of Zimbabwe's Hwange National Park. Lions are among the few predators, other than man, that will attack young elephants.*

Two young cheetahs
(Acinonyx jubatus) *survey the*
plains of Serengeti National
Park, Tanzania, from atop a
low mound.

Both the giraffe (Giraffa camelopardalis) *and the elephant have special adaptations for reaching high browse, but their anatomical solutions could not be more different. This is a reticulated giraffe in Kenya's Samburu Reserve.*

A leopard (Panthera pardus) *rests in a tree in Serengeti National Park, Tanzania.*

A trio of Cape ground squirrels (Xerus inauris) *sit up for a look around their arid homeland in the Namib-Naukluft Park, Namibia.*

Two springbok rams
(Antidorcas marsupialis) *spar*
in Namibia's Etosha Park.

A male warthog (Phacochoerus aethiopicus) *roots in the mud in Etosha Park, Namibia.*

A male Grant's gazelle (Gazella granti) *at Maasai Mara National Park, Kenya.*

105

A male anubis baboon (Papio anubis) *sits for his portrait in the Samburu Reserve, Kenya.*

Opposite:
The graceful gerenuk (Litocranius walleri) *is another high browser. Its long neck has earned it the alternate name of "giraffe-gazelle"; to reach even higher, it stands on its hind legs. This doe was photographed in the Samburu Reserve, Kenya.*

A flock of Egyptian geese (Alopochen aegyptiacus) *flies through the sunset at Chobe National Park, Botswana.*

A golden jackal (Canis aureus) *passes a flock of lesser flamingos* (Phoeniconaias minor) *in the shallows of a pond in the Ngorongoro Crater, Tanzania.*

109

A topi (Damaliscus lunatus) *and her calf scratch themselves in Kenya's Maasai Mara National Park.*

Elephants share the water hole with many smaller creatures, like this bull impala (Aepyceros melampus) *and his harem of seven cows photographed at Mana Pools National Park, Zimbabwe. They are doing one thing the elephant is incapable of: lowering their heads to the water to drink.*

One of the most striking of all birds of prey is the stub-tailed, long-winged bateleur (Terathopius ecaudatus). A widespread African species, this one was photographed in Chobe National Park, Botswana.

A young cow elephant encounters a gemsbok (Oryx gazella) beside a pool in Etosha Park, Namibia.

111

The red-faced mousebird
(Colius indicus) *is one of a*
group of six small, active,
long-tailed birds found only
in Africa. They have no near
relatives. Rather like
elephants, they are highly
social; members of a group
roost in a tightly packed
huddle. This one is at
Merondera, Zimbabwe.

Common, colorful and
conspicuous, the lilac-
breasted roller (Coracias
caudata) *is one of Africa's*
best-known birds. This one
is perched on a termite
mound on Fothergill Island,
Zimbabwe. Rollers get their
name from their acrobatic
courtship flights.

112

Bee-eaters are a common and beautiful feature of the African landscape. This one, photographed in Meru National Park, Kenya, is a blue-cheeked bee-eater (Merops persicus), *a winter visitor from Asia—one of many migrant birds that spend much of the year here.*

114

WITH ELEPHANTS
UNDERGROUND

IAN REDMOND

"ELEPHANT" AND "CAVE" ARE NOT WORDS THAT GO TOGETHER IN MOST PEOPLE'S minds. The very idea that elephants might burrow underground has the ring of one of those terrible schoolboy elephant jokes. And yet there is one place on earth where elephants do venture deep underground. They do it of their own volition, feeling their way with trunks outstretched, in total darkness, for hours at a time. Quite frankly, I could not believe my luck when I heard about this incredible phenomenon in 1980 and found that no one had studied it. Since then, during several field trips, I have spent nearly six months living in a cave called Kitum, watching and photographing elephants underground.

To understand what induces a normal African elephant to behave in such an unexpected fashion, it is necessary to understand something of the geology of the area they live in. The underground elephants are found on the forested slopes of Mount Elgon, a huge extinct volcano that sits astride the Kenya-Uganda border.

An area's ecology will always reflect its underlying geology. In East Africa, the geology is dominated by the Rift Valley, which is part of the three thousand-mile-long (5,000 km) Afro-Arabian Rift System, a series of parallel faults stretching from Mozambique northwards, via the Red Sea, to the Valley of Jordan. The faults result from pressure beneath the earth's crust that has caused the whole of East Africa to be thrust upwards. The resulting dome is punctuated by volcanoes and by flat-bottomed valleys, where long chunks of land have slipped down between the cracks.

A volcano that has become a sizable mountain begins to affect the local climate. As air currents rise up to pass over the summit, they cool, causing water vapor to condense as clouds and rain. When rain falls on the new rocks, it either runs off to form streams, or it soaks into the ground, depending on the nature of the volcano. An eruption of molten lava usually cools to form a dense rock such as basalt, which is impervious to water. But if the volcano also spewed out volcanic ash and other debris, this forms layers of lighter rocks such as tuffs and lapilli, through which

Two forest elephants (Loxodonta africana cyclotis) *sniff the air, almost hidden from sight in the dense* Hagenia *woodlands of Rwanda's Virunga Volcanoes. Forest elephants have more rounded ears and downward-pointing tusks than the bush elephant* (L. a. africana); *their scientific name,* cyclotis, *means "round-eared."*

115

rainwater can soak. As the water seeps through the rock, it dissolves out the soluble salts and carries them away in solution, either to the sea or, in some parts of the Rift Valley, to the soda lakes on the valley floor.

The rainfall will, in time, result in the growth of montane rainforests growing in soils that are leached of their soluble salts. Herbivores feeding in these forests have a problem. Their diet is deficient in salts, particularly sodium salts, which are necessary for an animal's physiological processes. Such animals are said to be "salt hungry," and their hunger for salt leads them to sample all kinds of novel food items, including earth and rock. Any exposure of salt-rich strata will soon become known to salt-hungry herbivores, and they will visit this natural salt lick daily, or as the need dictates, to eat the earth.

The concentration of wildlife visible around naturally occurring salt licks has led to the building of tourist lodges beside some of them. At The Ark in Kenya's Aberdares National Park, for example, visitors are treated to the sight of shy forest antelopes such as bushbuck, duikers and even on occasion bongo, out in the open, daintily nibbling and licking the earth. Hyenas and leopards are also sometimes seen around salt licks; it is not the salt that attracts them, however, but the animals eating it. Predators have no need to eat earth because their meat comes ready-salted. In a food chain, a deficit need only be rectified once.

Although elephants also visit salt licks, they cannot lick the salt. An elephant's tongue cannot reach around its trunk and tusks, and so a salt-hungry elephant uses its tusks to dig up clods of earth, which it places in its mouth with the tip of the trunk. The amount of soil that an elephant ingests is remarkable. Trunkful after trunkful is lifted up, chewed briefly and then swallowed. After observing a young bull elephant at The Ark for 45 minutes, Hezy Shoshani calculated that it must have eaten about 37.5 pounds (17 kg) of earth!

This digging behavior is the key to understanding the cave elephants of Mount Elgon. The walls of the Elgon caves are composed of salt-rich volcanic tuffs, which are soft enough to be chiselled with a tusk. These subterranean salt licks are visited by all the salt-hungry antelopes, buffaloes and elephants that dwell in the Elgon forests. But perhaps the most remarkable aspect of the caves is the question of how they were formed.

There are untold numbers of caves hidden away in the forested valleys of Elgon's flanks. Most of those that have been explored conform to a similar pattern: they are cul-de-sacs extending more or less horizontally into the mountain, usually behind a waterfall that cascades over a cliff, the top edge of which forms the leading edge of an old lava flow. The pattern of these caves does not fit that of caves formed by the usual processes of cave formation. River-eroded caves have more than one opening. There was never a sea or large lake at this altitude, around 8,000 feet (2,438 m) on Elgon, so wave erosion cannot be responsible. The Elgon caves cannot be lava tubes because they are the wrong shape, and they lie beneath the lava layer, not in it. Many of the caves have been enlarged by the El Kony people, sometimes known as the Elgon Maasai, who used to dig out rock to feed to their salt-hungry cattle. However, the low, man-made chambers are easily identified as later additions to the main chambers.

The question of how the caves were formed has perplexed visitors to Elgon for more than a century. The Scottish explorer Joseph Thomson was the first white man to explore the region in 1883. He noted that some

IAN REDMOND

of the caves were inhabited, but the people who dwelt there pointed to their primitive tools and laughed at his suggestion that the huge caverns could have been excavated by their forefathers. Some visitors have commented that the elephants must have enlarged parts of the existing caves when tusking the walls. The results of my research, however, seem to support another more radical hypothesis — that the caves have been dug largely by generations of salt-hungry elephants. It seems to me that these are not just caves into which elephants go, but ancient elephant salt mines, which are still being worked to this day.

How prevalent is this novel geological process — "erosion by elephant"? Can the presence of mammoth or mastodon bones and dung in caves be explained by subterranean salt digging? Could the folk tales of mammoths living in caves have a ring of truth? The fact that elephants dig for salt is well known. On most East African mountains there are signs of salt-hungry elephants. Roadside cuttings in the Aberdares, or on Mounts Kenya and Kilimanjaro, are often marked by tuskings, where the curve of a living ivory chisel has sliced through the earth. Natural cliffs of mineral-rich rock may also be scraped by tusks up to a height of fourteen feet (4.3 m), often creating an overhang. In Tanzania, on the outer slopes of Ngorongoro Crater, a short walk from Gibbs Farm (a popular tourist retreat), there are some small elephant caves, extending a few yards into the steep bank of a stream. They are not deep enough to have a dark zone, and when I visited them in 1985 the front of the cave mouth had recently collapsed. Elephants had subsequently been eating the roof-fall, and it was clear that over time elephant erosion here would result in a receding cliff.

A bull elephant digs at the earth of a salt lick, using his tusks to pry up clods of earth that he will then place in his mouth with his trunk and eat.

117

It was in the Virunga Volcanoes, where I studied mountain gorillas with the late Dian Fossey, that I first saw signs of this phenomenon. On the northern slopes of Mount Mikeno, in Zaire, there is a cliff known to elephants and gorillas as a source of salt. Long before I had a research interest in the subject, I marvelled at how the elephants' tusks had sculpted the rockface into bumps and hollows, shaped according to the relative softness of the strata. We would occasionally find gorilla dung full of grit and small stones following a visit to this or other mineral-rich sites.

It was also here that I first encountered elephants. The Virunga elephants are of the forest sub-species, which are smaller than bush elephants, with smaller, more rounded ears and downwards pointing, brownish-yellow tusks. Only a pitiful few have survived the ivory poachers, and so it is a rarity to see elephants at all, even when walking daily through the forest to locate the gorillas. I'll always remember the excitement of my first close encounter.

We glimpsed them from about thirty paces away, quietly feeding in a sunny glade. My Rwandan tracker, Nemeye, was very cautious, and thought I was crazy wanting to move closer. He said that it was no use climbing a tree because if the elephant was angry, it would push the tree over to get at you. If the tree was too big, it would put its trunk into its mouth and draw out water with which it would squirt you off the branches. This, I thought, I've got to see. We climbed into a massive Hagenia tree and I began waving and shouting, "Nzovu! Gweno hano!" (Kinyarwanda for "Elephant! Come here!"). I tried it in Swahili, French and English, but the most reaction I got was a couple of ear flaps and a slight waving of the trunk in our general direction before they resumed their feeding. Nevertheless, it was a red-letter day for me.

That evening, my story of the day's adventure prompted Dian to reminisce about the herd of elephants that used to visit the stream that flows through the Karisoke Research Centre, to drink and bathe. She told me how, once, she had come face to face with a young elephant around a bend in the trail. Both were startled and Dian was not at all sure how to react, so she raised her arms above her head and began to sway her hips in a sort of music-hall belly dance, with vocal accompaniment. The elephant calf looked perplexed, stuck out its ears and backed off. Dian collapsed in adrenalin-fed giggles. Sadly, the last member of that herd was shot for its tusks in 1975, the year before I joined her at the Karisoke Research Centre.

Exciting though it was, that first elephant experience was as nothing compared to those that followed when I began to study elephants in caves. My sense of wonder had as much to do with the setting as with the animals themselves. Picture yourself on a ledge in a cave-mouth, with a waterfall splashing on moss-covered rocks. Suddenly, the moonlit forest vibrates with a deep, elephantine rumble: the miners are here. Slowly and cautiously, trunks snaking at the whiff of human, they pace in a single file along the familiar trail and up the steep entrance path. Then, one by one, they disappear into the deeper gloom of Kitum Cave.

Once the elephants became accustomed to the idea of a "tame" human moving about the rocks, I hoped that they would tolerate my presence in the back of the cave. They did. If they entered despite knowing I was there, I would follow them in, darting across the entrance and keeping to the low part of the cave out of reach of blindly wandering pachyderms. To find my way, I would keep my fingers over a small flash-

IAN REDMOND

light, allowing just a sliver of light to shine along the ground. Once inside, I could climb onto a jumbled pile of fallen roof and look along the flashlight's beam to make my observations. The sights are indelibly printed in my mind—elephants feeling their way around boulders bigger than themselves and splashing through pools, the cows keeping a protective trunk on their calves, and all the while, above their backs, fruit bats swinging free of their roost and circling overhead, eyes gleaming in the faint light.

The bizarre combination of bats and elephants amidst the stark rocks of the cave made the scene almost surreal. The experience was heightened by switching off the flashlight. In total darkness the other senses strain for information, and you begin to get some idea of how the cave feels to an elephant. First come the sounds. With a stereo cassette recorder, I taped one of the strangest sound pictures ever to be broadcast by the BBC. The high-pitched twittering and squealing of the bats was countered by deep elephant rumbles that reverberated around the cave. The clunk and thud of tusk on rock would be followed by the amazing sound of massive molars crunching and grinding the lumps of rock.

Touch is also a sense that comes into its own as you feel your way through the darkness. The textures of the cave vary from the sharp-edged flakes of harder rock to the crumbly layers of tuff, but over much of the floor, unexpectedly, your feet register a soft carpet. This is composed of the accumulated dung of untold generations of elephants, liberally sprinkled with the more liquid fecal deposits of thousands of fruit bats. A large umbrella would be useful if you plan to take photographs underneath the bat roost, and be careful not to leave your camera pointing upwards for too long. The result of this scatological carpet is an olfactory onslaught that has to be sniffed to be believed!

Giant groundsels (Senecio johnstonii) *dot the alpine grasslands of Mount Elgon, home of the unique "cave elephants."*

119

In single file, a herd of elephants feels its way into the darkness of Kitum Cave.

For a visually oriented species like *Homo sapiens* to fully appreciate the cave, however, it is necessary to explore it with lights when there are no elephants present. This is what I first did in 1980, with Mike Carter, a friend who was a surveyor. In mapping Kitum, we discovered that the back wall is 175 yards (160 m) from the entrance, and the cave is 45 yards (41 m) wide at its mouth, widening to more than 100 yards across in the bat chamber. At that time the roof was supported by a huge pillar of rock, but in 1982, probably as a result of a slight earth tremor, the back third of the cave collapsed. The ceiling is now much higher over where the pillar once stood, and an enormous pile of rubble and massive slabs of rock forms a new obstacle. No longer able to reach the deepest mining bays, the elephants are gradually finding ways over the new mound to tusk at the freshly exposed roof.

It was beside the pillar, the year before its collapse, that I had my first sight of an elephant deep underground. From our sleeping ledge in the cave mouth, my wife Caroline and I heard elephants entering the cave just after dusk. Once the entrance seemed clear, I crept in after them, all senses alert. In the darkness I could hear the whoosh of air down a trunk, and the occasional clunk of tusk on rock. Huge boulders that I had mapped earlier, glimpsed now out of the corner of my eye, suddenly seemed alarmingly like elephant bottoms. I froze, and then, determined to see a *real* underground elephant, continued to feel my way onto the pile of old roof-fall. From this high point, I cautiously shone a thin beam around the cave. Then it happened. A dusty brown forehead appeared around the side of the pillar. It was a young bull, probably in his early teens. He seemed to

120

IAN REDMOND

Erosion by elephant in action: an elephant scrapes at the walls of Kitum Cave with its tusks. Ian Redmond is convinced that over thousands of years such behavior actually created the caves on Mount Elgon.

glide past, within a few yards of where I crouched, apparently oblivious to the flashlight. So slowly did he place each foot down, that I felt as though I were watching an old sepia film being shown in slow motion. He climbed onto the mound of fallen roof, steering clear of a deep crevasse, and then paused for several minutes before heading out into the night. This encounter did much to increase my confidence about following the elephants underground. I realized then that aggressive charges towards me were unlikely, given the elephants' need to feel their way slowly around dangerous obstacles. As an agile primate with a flashlight, I definitely had the upper hand, and soon discovered that as long as I kept a low profile and did not shine too much light, I could record their behavior without affecting it unduly.

Further observations soon followed, and with them a number of surprises. Caroline and I had anticipated that the elephants would be nervous about entering such a strange environment, and that they would spend as little time as possible underground. Besides, the back of the cave is so dark that, even during the day, you cannot see your hand, or your trunk, in front of your face. It would be logical, we thought, for the elephants to utilize the entrance chamber during daylight hours, so that they could at least see what they were doing. We were wrong on all counts. We found that most visits to the cave took place after dark and that a visit might last for hours on end. At dusk, the shadowy shapes of elephant families would emerge from the forest and be swallowed up by the black maw of Kitum. Family herds would walk in line, trunk to tail like circus elephants, to avoid any youngsters straying into danger. The adults knew, I am sure, that the crevasse in the old pile of fallen roof had, at some time in the past, claimed the lives of at least two calves and several antelopes. One wrong foot in the dark would mean a slow agonizing death.

Once past the crevasse, however, the elephants would spread out across the back chamber and begin mining. They then seemed completely at ease, tusking at walls and roof-fall alike, and even tolerating an occasional flash photograph. With direct observation, still photographs, and film taken by a television documentary crew using infra-red light and an image intensifier, much of their underground behavior was revealed. One flash caught a cow throwing dust over herself; I watched another calmly suckling her calf beside the pillar; two teenage bulls were seen one night, play-fighting and sparring. All were examples of perfectly normal elephant behavior, but unique in that they were being acted out up to 175 yards (160 m) inside a cave, in total darkness.

To find out how long the elephants would spend underground, I varied my observation techniques a little. I was concerned that my presence in the back of the cave might precipitate an early departure, so on some nights I just recorded their time of entry and departure. Afterwards, by checking the piles of dung (the warm ones are the fresh ones), I could tell which part of the cave they had mined. To our amazement, it turned out that they sometimes spent five or six hours inside the cave. Knowing that elephants normally spend about 80 percent of each twenty-four hours feeding, this seemed an unreasonably long time to be lurking about in a leafless cave. What, we wanted to know, were they doing in there for so long?

To find out, I set up the cassette recorder in the crevasse, with the microphones sticking up into the cave, and ran a length of black cotton thread from there, back down the low south side, to the cave mouth. With one hand running along the thread, and one hand outstretched at head height, I could then creep into the cave after the elephants had entered, without shining any lights that might affect their behavior. At first, there would be sounds of movement, occasional rumbles, and the sounds of them mining and eating rock. After an hour or so, elephant sounds would become less and less frequent. Most of the bats had left by that time, and apart from the distant splattering of the waterfall over the cave mouth, there were few sounds for the microphones to pick up. I would begin to wonder whether the elephants had tiptoed out, leaving me alone. Fortunately, certain involuntary sounds would reassure me that they were still there. For most of the preceding day, these elephants would have been feeding in the forest. Their digestive processes, as anyone who has eaten too many greens will know, tend to produce quantities of gas. As a result, flatulence is not uncommon and this is how the BBC sound archive comes to have in its collection stereophonic recordings of elephantine farts, echoing through the darkness of Kitum Cave.

But the question remains, what are they doing so quietly in there when not breaking wind? Unlikely as it seems, the answer appears to be sleeping. Elephants that were studied around the clock in Uganda, by other researchers, were found to sleep for from one to four hours each night, usually between 3:00 and 7:00 A.M. Although cave visits were usually earlier than that, the Elgon elephants may decide to stay underground to sleep because of the cave's temperature. Enter the cave on a sunny day, and the interior feels cool and dank. But if you stay inside until after dark,

IAN REDMOND

The elephants may have dug Kitum, but they are not the only animals to use it. Here a bushbuck (Tragelaphus scriptus) *steps gingerly along a ledge as it descends into the cave in search of salt.*

you really notice the chill night air on departure. At this altitude on the mountain, night temperatures in the forest can drop to within a few degrees of freezing, whereas the back of the cave remains a constant 57°F (14°C). The fact that the caves we monitored were not visited every night suggests that finding a warm bedroom is not the main reason the elephants go underground. Nevertheless, their subterranean slumbers do explain why, once inside, they stay so long in there.

The decisions in a family herd of elephants are made by the matriarch, and so it is she who decides when it is time to leave the cave. Her sisters, daughters and their offspring may be spread out all over the cave snoozing, splashing in pools, or still mining, but somehow the matriarch must gather them all together into an orderly procession. Usually, before a herd left the cave, I would hear a stunning roar, which filled the cave with solid sound, and which I felt with my skin as much as heard with my ears. This I took to be a sort of rallying call. In the silence that followed, I could often hear the soft scrape of hide on rock, the splash of footsteps through pools, and then another sound, the sound of rough hides rubbing together as the elephants gathered prior to climbing up over the mound of old rooffall. This was the dangerous bit, avoiding the crevasse again, and yet I saw a large cow — the matriarch I presumed — shoving and butting a younger elephant into the lead position. Was she ensuring that her offspring learned the layout of the cave? Or simply using her authority to get out of the chore of feeling for a safe way over the mound? I did get the distinct impression that the elephant-miners have some sort of mental map of the cave layout, in much the same way that blind people become familiar with the location of their furniture and local amenities. On one occasion I watched a confident young bull on his way out; he speeded up as he climbed onto the mound, casting his trunk forwards every couple of steps as if just making sure of a path he already knew.

It was one such young bull, an adolescent who had declined to heed the rallying call of the matriarch, who gave me my clearest observations of the mining technique. He was working, head down, in a low side chamber, which could barely accommodate an adult elephant. The cave floor here was deep mud, from the back-flow of the waterfall, but enough boulders of harder rock had been tusked out from the ceiling to form slippery stepping stones. Clutching my flashlight, camera and flash unit, I cautiously hopped from rock to rock until I could see what he was doing.

With his trunk tip he was feeling for irregularities in the rock; then he would place the tip of his ivory chisel against a likely bump and, with the benefit of his four- or five-ton bulk, push hard. As the rock gave way, the tusk would gouge another polished stripe across the wall or ceiling, and Charles (as this bull came to be known) would have to try to catch the rock fragments with his trunk before they plopped into the knee-deep mud in which he stood. This was clearly a tricky operation in total darkness, and although he tolerated my attentions for several minutes, after the fourth (and closest) flash photograph, Charles decided to get rid of the photographer. He turned, stretched to his full height and spread his ears in an impressive visual display, which wouldn't have been much good in the dark if I hadn't had my flashlight on him. As it was, there was enough light to convince me that discretion should be the better part of elephant watching. I fired off one last shot, and hopped backwards out of his way (I was standing in the only exit from that side chamber). To my surprise, instead of leaving at that point, he came out of the side chamber and went deeper into the main cave. I circled round to sit on the steep rock face above him, and trained a flashlight on him as he searched out fragments of freshly broken roof-fall. He was deftly moving larger rocks with his forefeet, and feeling beneath them with his trunk tip for bite-sized morsels. The grinding and slurping was clearly audible, and his nimble footwork in the beam of my flashlight brought to mind the image of an overweight song and dance man in a spotlight, chomping his way through another soft-shoe shuffle.

Charles spent more than one hour eating roof-fall that night, and that was on top of his earlier mining in the side chamber. It is impossible to quantify accurately how much rock was carried out of the cave in his belly, but a conservative estimate would be in the region of a one-gallon bucketful (4.5 L) (volume is more useful than weight in this calculation). An order of magnitude calculation puts erosion by elephant, as a geological process, into perspective: the volume of the Kitum main cave is just under seven million gallons (30 000 000 L or 30 000 m³), which means that at Charles' rate of excavation alone, it would take less than 20,000 years to excavate Kitum — a mere blink of the eye in terms of geological time-scales. Although this is clearly not an exact figure, it does demonstrate that a cave like Kitum could be excavated over a few tens of thousands of years. It is several million years since Elgon last erupted; African elephants have been around for the past five million years; and those that dwelt in salt-deficient areas, such as Mount Elgon, would have exhibited normal elephant salt-digging behavior. But why did this result in spectacular caverns on Mount Elgon and nowhere else? According to my "elephant speleogenesis" hypothesis, it is because of a geological peculiarity.

As the layers of Elgon's volcanic ash were worn away by wind and rain, the downhill edges of the harder lava flows were left standing high, until each formed the lip of a cliff. Where streams flowed, small valleys were formed, and the lip of each cliff became a waterfall. Once the height of such a cliff became greater than the depth of the lava, the layer of ash beneath the lava would have been exposed. This would still be rich in soluble salts, because the impervious lava acted as a rock umbrella to keep out the rain. Any such exposure would soon become known to salt-hungry herbivores, and the cliff on either side of the waterfall would feel the effects of a new form of erosion: nibbling teeth, licking tongues and, most of all, digging tusks.

The cliff would become an overhang, and then a cave, just as in other

A. SUTCLIFFE

The tip of an Elgon elephant's tusk, scratched and worn from years of digging for salt.

localities. But this is where Elgon's lava layers make the situation unique. When the first roof-fall occurs, it does not affect the tough lava lip of the cliff above the cave. Each new pile of fallen rock is within the cave and only affects the rate or direction of excavation; over time the cave continues to grow, held up by the strong lava roof. In fact, if the fallen rock inside is salty, it too will be excavated; hence the floor of the chamber gradually returns to its former level but with a higher ceiling. This process may account for the spectacular rock arch that forms the entrance chamber of Mackingeni Cave, over which cascades a slender one-hundred-foot (30.5 m) waterfall.

Two caves I have visited demonstrate the final stages of the life of an elephant cave. The entrance chamber had collapsed completely, lava and all. Access to the rear chambers was then only possible through the cracked roof, after climbing over the jumble of overgrown lava blocks and slabs that are inhabited by hordes of hyrax. The rocks around these broken entrances are grooved with the gnawing of thousands of hyrax teeth because they, like their distant cousins the elephants, are salt-hungry herbivores.

The elephants, however, pay a high price for their ration of salt. Their tusks are unnaturally short. Mining the rock wears down the ivory faster than it can grow, and many elephants on Mount Elgon have stumpy tusks, which barely protrude beyond the base of the trunk. For this reason, I did not fear unduly for my study animals; ivory poaching was not a problem on Elgon, and I was free to concentrate purely on research. As the elephants came to accept my presence, so I came to respect their remarkable intelligence. I began to appreciate the extent to which elephant behavior is determined by learning rather than instinct. A baby elephant learns from its parents and elders where to find food, drink, salt, and other necessities. This knowledge is passed down from generation to generation, and each population, or tribe, of elephants benefits from the accumulated experience and wisdom of its forebears — what in human tribes we refer to as culture.

125

This bull drinking in Amboseli National Park, Kenya, shows how different individual elephants can be from each other: his tusks are asymmetrical, and he appears unusually small-eared and pot-bellied.

The use of the caves is a feature of Elgon elephant culture, and this accounts for the elephants' relaxed behavior underground. To the human observer, an elephant in a cave is a weird and unnatural sight; however, to an Elgon elephant, venturing underground is something learned at his or her mother's knee. From their earliest days, calves accompany their mothers underground. They learn the layout of the caves and, when they are weaned, they learn how to mine for salt. To them, this behavior is normal. They do not know that they are the only troglodyte tuskers in the world.

But why do they not simply tusk the rock near the cave mouth? What induces them to search the farthest corners of the cave? It may be that the behavior we see today is the result of an unbroken line of instruction dating back to the original cliff-diggers. No single generation would notice much difference in the size of their caves, but as the centuries passed, the overhangs grew into deep salt mines, and the cliff-diggers became miners.

Sadly, however, the miners' days are numbered. Despite the worn-down tusks and the protection offered by being in a national park, the high price of ivory in the mid 1980s led to heavy poaching. Such was the demand for ivory around the world that even the tusks of the Elgon elephants were considered profitable. As a result, since 1986, most of my study animals have been shot. Family herds were ambushed throughout the park, often while making their way into a cave. The weapons used were small-caliber machine guns. The poachers were not marksmen, aiming for the big tuskers; they simply sprayed their bullets into the terrified animals so that, eventually, vital organs were hit. Some elephants staggered a few hundred yards, pursued by the poachers; others escaped, wounded, to die days or weeks afterwards. It was brutal slaughter.

Although reports of the poaching filtered out in 1986, it was not until 1987 that my other commitments allowed me to return to the park. It was worse than I had imagined. The rutted, muddy tracks seemed normal, and as I drove along I longed for a glimpse of an elephantine back in the dense undergrowth. It was on the bend below Kitum Cave that the stench hit my nostrils—the sickening stench of rotting flesh. It hung heavily beneath the trees, violating the beauty of the sunlit forest and permeating every pore. It grew stronger, then faded, leaving a lingering taste in the back of my mouth. Near the path up to Kitum Cave, the same thing happened again, but I put off the unpleasant task that lay in store. The sun was

126

sinking quickly behind the mountain, and, alone, it could have taken some time to locate the decomposing animals. I shouldered my pack and walked up to the cave to settle in on the familiar rocky ledge before dark.

No elephants visited the cave that night, and there were no signs of fresh mining activity. The next morning I drove around the lower circuits of the park track and was relieved to find fresh droppings from the previous night. An adult elephant had been tusking a roadside cutting in search of salt, and a half-chewed branch had been dropped in the middle of the road. There were still some elephants left, thank goodness, but how many? And why were they tusking beside the road, rather than in the caves? I drove down to the park headquarters to hear the warden's bad news. Since February 1986 there had been heavy poaching for ivory. Poachers apparently came from both sides of the Kenya-Uganda border, but it was clear that the automatic weapons were leftovers from the civil unrest in Uganda. By June 1986 the situation had become so serious that the warden felt obliged to close the park to the public and bring in reinforcements from the Kenyan army and police. Even helicopters were used on occasion.

The park remained closed to the public for three months, and by the end of 1986 things were looking better. Between January and March 1987, eleven poachers were captured and imprisoned. The warden replaced some of the dilapidated log bridges, and one ford, with sturdy concrete bridges, and he greatly improved some of the park roads. A special anti-poaching unit was stationed in the park. However, poaching attacks were still taking place, and the protection of the park and its elephants was hampered by a simple lack of funds for fuel, vehicle repairs and maintenance. Forty-two carcasses had been found since the poaching began, but no one knew how many lay hidden in Elgon's forested valleys. And no one knew how many elephants had survived.

After hearing the warden's report, I went with one of the rangers to see the result of the latest attack. We pushed through the undergrowth for 50 paces or so before finding the first carcass. A heaving torrent of maggots spilled out from under the thick brown skin. The bones had been scattered randomly by the larger scavengers. I was surprised to see that the elephant's skull was not much bigger than a basketball. It was a calf of perhaps three and a half years of age. The tusks, which were recovered, were the size of a man's thumb. What a bloody waste.

The second body was larger — a young male of about fifteen years. The skull showed that his whole face had been cut off in a single plane, apparently confirming rumors that the poachers came equipped with a chain saw for speedy removal of the tusks. It occurred to me that this might be Charles. There was no way I could be sure, but the age was about right, and the mere possibility sent my mind racing. Standing beside the mutilated body, I felt the same gut-wrenching surge of sadness and anger that accompanied my discovery of Digit's body nearly ten years before. Digit was the young silverback mountain gorilla whose death, at the hands of poachers, triggered the highly successful Mountain Gorilla Project and Digit Fund, which together have ensured a future for what Dian Fossey called "the greatest of the great apes." Whether this was Charles rotting at my feet became irrelevant. The fact was, someone had shot another of my study animals and sawn off his face. Why? To supply a mindless market among the wealthy for ivory trinkets and bangles. There had to be something I could do to help prevent this carnage.

With the help of BBC *Wildlife* magazine, I launched an appeal — The African Ele-Fund — in November 1987. Not wishing to form yet another organization in the already crowded field of conservation, the Ele-Fund operates through several existing groups. It has quickly grown into an international network of some of the best-known wildlife charities and conservation organizations. I am grateful to all of them because, without exception, they have allowed me to appeal to their members and then handled all donations with absolutely no deductions for administration. This has enabled 100 percent of every donation to be used for conservation work. Urgently needed funds have been sent to purchase or repair vehicles and equipment, and to monitor elephant populations in Kenya, Tanzania and Namibia. In 1989 Ele-Fund joined with Care for the Wild, World Society for the Protection of Animals and Zoo Check to launch the ELEFRIENDS campaign, which has resulted in the declaration of ELEFRIENDLY ZONES all over the world, where ivory is not welcome. Demonstrations were organized and more than one million people signed a pledge not to wear, buy, sell or display ivory.

How many elephants survived on Mount Elgon? In 1988 Hezy Shoshani and I made a brief census by counting droppings and by questioning park rangers and local farmers. We even tried flying low over the forest. The purpose of the flight, however, was not to count the elephants but to locate them, in order to make follow-up observations on foot. Conventional aerial counts of elephants, as practiced over the African savannah, are not possible in a forest habitat because the ground is mostly hidden under the canopy of leaves. But in patchy montane rainforest, such as that which clothes the slopes of Mount Elgon, at least a few members of a herd are likely to be spotted. Even if the elephants themselves remain hidden, the branches broken off where they have been feeding, their huge, water-filled footprints, or even their football-sized droppings, are normally visible in open clearings. As we quartered the ground in the small plane we saw many smaller species: a buffalo crashed away through a thicket; solitary forest antelopes stood, tense and nervous, in glades as we passed overhead; from the height we were flying, even the hyrax were clearly visible, scuttling over the rocks and diving for cover. But of elephants we saw no sign at all.

Because of the difficulties in counting elephants — dead or alive — in dense forest, no accurate figures exist for Elgon. It is clear, however, that there has been a drastic decline. In the early 1970s John Wreford-Smith, a naturalist who then lived on Elgon, estimated that there were about 1,200 elephants on the Kenya side, but none on the Uganda side of the mountain. Between 1980 and 1985, during my field trips, it was unusual to drive through the park and not see fresh signs of elephants, if not the animals themselves. In 1988 we came up with a range of estimates between 100 and 400, and I fear the lower end was more likely.

If we just sit back and let the ivory poachers finish their bloody work, it is not just another population of elephants we will have lost. The whole spectacle of elephants in caves, which we have barely begun to understand, would disappear. Even if, at some future time, elephants were reintroduced to Elgon's forests, there would be no guarantee that they would enter the caves. If the world had not decided to ban the ivory trade, I have no doubt at all that Elgon's unique elephants would have been wiped out.

Where elephants have been exterminated, bushy thickets can choke out more open areas, destroying habitat for grassland animals. At normal population densities, elephants, like this bull in the Zambesi Valley, Zimbabwe, open up the undergrowth and create a patchwork environment that provides habitats for a large number of plants and animals.

As it is, they have a chance providing the ban is not lifted in 1992. Attitudes are changing towards ivory. Thanks to public awareness campaigns such as ELEFRIENDS, ivory is no longer seen as a desirable status symbol, but as a rather gruesome relic of a bygone era. If this change in attitude can be effected among all those who have bought, or would buy, ivory, then the poaching will stop. The bottom line for the criminals who shoot elephants, and who murder anyone who interferes with their dirty business, is whether the trade is profitable. Without the financial incentive, the poachers, smugglers and dealers would turn their attentions elsewhere.

What has happened on Elgon is a microcosm of events over much of Africa. Things have improved since the ivory ban, but poaching is not yet finished. Seven elephants are known to have been killed in 1990, and one ranger was shot dead when his patrol was ambushed. The ivory dealers appear to be keeping operations ticking over at a low level, probably in the hope that the ban will be relaxed before long, and illegal ivory will once more find its way into outlets for legal ivory. Fortunately, Mount Elgon National Park has just been increased to 3.5 times its former size by the Kenyan government, and a fund-raising drive has been launched to help pay for the cost of protecting the increased area. All the forests and the Afro-alpine moorlands on the Kenya side of Mount Elgon now have the highest level of legal protection, with national park status. Underground elephant viewing has the potential to be a major attraction for the discerning ecotourist. With careful planning and controls, small parties of tourists would not only experience a unique phenomenon, but would also ensure that the elephants are seen to be worth more alive than dead.

The Elgon elephant tribe has more of a future now than at any time in the past twenty years, but if the ivory trade is legalized again, the poaching will recommence. How long then before the forests and caves no longer reverberate with the matriarch's rallying call?

AT THE WATER'S EDGE

Whether they live in the desert or the rainforest, water is a constant in elephants' lives. The daily visit to a water hole, river, or pool is not just an opportunity to drink. At the water's edge, elephants bathe, wallow in the mud, graze on soft aquatic plants. Waterside activities form an important part of elephant social life, and in the dry season courtship and mating take place among the breeding herds clustered at their drinking sites. Here, too, elephants encounter many of the other creatures with which they share the African wilderness.

Elephants like this bull at the edge of the Zambesi River in Zimbabwe approach water not just to drink, but also to graze on sedges and other plants. Old bulls prefer to feed on soft emergent plants; they often died by the water's edge, and their accumulated remains gave rise to the myth of the elephant graveyard.

This handsome cow from Etosha National Park, Namibia, may be able to take up nine quarts (10.5 L) of water with each trunkful. Her calf can probably manage about three quarts (3.5 L). Notice the peaked forehead characteristic of female African elephants.

Caked with dust, a bull stands knee-deep in a pan at Chobe, his trunk tip floating on the surface.

Two Etosha calves, with and without the effects of a mud wallow. A coating of mud protects an elephant's skin from insect bites and the direct rays of the sun, and its moisture helps keep the skin cool.

133

A bull herd crosses a pool in Mana Pools National Park, Zimbabwe.

*A herd drinks from a pan
at Etosha National Park,
Namibia.*

The daily visit to a water hole provides an opportunity for play for these young calves in Etosha Park, Namibia.

A muddy young bull in Hwange National Park, Zimbabwe, fills his throat with a trunkful of water.

136

A bull elephant uses its trunk as a portable shower hose. A spray of water will help to cool his skin.

Following pages:
Two bulls in Botswana's Chobe National Park drink their fill at a pan.

Elephants, like these bulls climbing onto an island in the Zambesi River, Zimbabwe, swim well and will enter deep water; they have even crossed Lake Kariba, a distance of 30 miles (48 km). Notice the rounded forehead profile typical of bulls.

Few African mammals are so thoroughly tied to water as is the hippopotamus. This one, in Maasai Mara National Park in Kenya, has a passenger: a yellow-billed oxpecker (Buphagus africana), a species of starling. Oxpeckers ride many large mammals, feeding on ticks and other insects, but they avoid elephants, who may not tolerate them.

141

INSET: RICK WEYERHAEUSER/WORLD WILDLIFE FUND

AFTERWORD

RONALD ORENSTEIN

THE STORY OF THE ELEPHANT CRISIS HAS BEEN A STIRRING TALE OF remarkable individuals, people like the authors of this book. There are others working in Africa: Garth Owen-Smith, who is fighting a battle against South African bureaucracy in his fight to save the desert elephants of Namibia; Cynthia Moss and Joyce Poole, who have lived for years among the elephants of Amboseli National Park, learning their ways; Daphne Sheldrick, whose orphanage for elephants and rhinos in Kenya has attracted world-wide attention; Costa Mlay, who spearheaded one of Africa's most successful antipoaching drives in Tanzania; and many more, some well-known, others—including the dedicated rangers who risk their lives every day in the war against the poachers—unknown and, perhaps, unrewarded.

Most of you reading this book live in a country without wild elephants. The problems of poaching, the intricacies of the African environment and the fabric of its society may seem far away, untouchable, unreachable. You may feel that there is little you can do about them. In fact, there is a great deal you can do. You have already started by buying this book, and thus supporting the International Wildlife Coalition's scholarship program for the children of game wardens in Tanzania.

The important thing to remember is that your help for the African elephant and the land it occupies is not just possible; it is, in fact, vital. What is more, it is a debt we owe.

We owe that debt not only because of the pleasure and excitement that elephants—whether alive, on film or tape, or in stories—have given us. We owe it because the problems that the elephant faces exist, to a very great extent, because of the intrusion of the West into the African world. Overpopulation and habitat destruction at the pace we see them today are at least partly the result of technologies and economic schemes that have been transplanted into Africa from the developed nations. The poachers that slaughtered the elephant herds were armed with Kalashnikovs and AK-47s that arms suppliers poured into Africa during its civil wars. The

Will there be living elephants in a future Africa—or only the mutilated carcasses left by poachers as mute testament to our folly and greed? The choice is ours.

143

ivory trade flourished because we, in the wealthy nations of the world, found ivory beautiful and desirable. We were prepared to pay high prices for it, and unwilling to think of the magnificent creatures from which it was torn.

You do not have to be a world-renowned authority, a scientist or international politician, to pay that debt. It is amazing what even the smallest effort can accomplish. When I began campaigning against the ivory trade in Canada in 1989, on behalf of the International Wildlife Coalition, I sent some information on what was happening to the elephant to a number of stores and asked them to withdraw ivory from their shelves. I didn't expect much in the way of response; and yet three major Canadian chains—Birks, Sears and The Bay—agreed without argument to stop selling ivory. Birks recalled and wrote off over $80,000 worth of ivory merchandise. That was the effect of one letter! Afterwards, I helped to organize the African Elephant Emergency Network, which lobbied the Canadian government to ban ivory imports and achieved its goal in just six weeks. A single committed person—like you—is far from helpless.

So what can you do? The obvious thing, of course, is to stop buying ivory. You may think that that is unnecessary advice. However, it is not illegal to sell ivory. There is a great deal of misunderstanding about the current international ban on the ivory trade. The CITES treaty, under which the ban was passed, deals only in international trade. It comes into play only when wildlife, or products made from that wildlife, cross international borders. Importing and exporting ivory for commercial purposes is illegal for a CITES party that has not taken a reservation against the ban, but the sale of ivory is not.

Remember, too, that the ban itself may not last. It will certainly be attacked at the next CITES meeting. The smugglers, poachers and ivory dealers are still hoping that the ivory trade is not dead, but only sleeping. They are even stockpiling ivory in anticipation of the day that the profits from this terrible trade rise once again.

So, I repeat: never buy ivory. You have made ivory unfashionable, and the most important thing that you can do for the African elephant is to keep up the good work.

In fact, that advice applies not only for the elephant, but also for other ivory-producing animals like the walrus and narwhal, which are already feeling the poacher's hand. It may even apply to an animal no conservationist can help — the woolly mammoth. Mammoth ivory is surprisingly common on the Siberian tundra. Since the ban, a brisk trade in mammoth ivory has sprung up. That wouldn't be a problem, except that some mammoth ivory is very hard to distinguish from elephant ivory. There have already been a few cases in the United States of people smuggling in elephant ivory by claiming that it came from a mammoth. Mammoth ivory is often easy to spot — it can be orange or brown, and is often cracked in many places—but if you are not sure, play it safe and don't buy it.

If you can afford it, you might consider helping the elephant earn revenue for Africa as a living animal, by visiting the continent as an ecotourist. There are many tours available. As well as enjoying an unforgettable experience, you will be helping the elephant justify itself economically to a poor land. After you return, consider writing a letter to the Wildlife Ministry of the country you visited, expressing your appreciation and thanking them for their efforts to conserve their wildlife.

You can also use your power as a voter to help the elephant. The International Wildlife Coalition, for example, is trying to convince the government of Canada to ban the sale of ivory outright, and in the United States we have petitioned the government to list the African elephant under the Endangered Species Act. You can encourage your representatives to support these or similar measures. However, Africa needs more than an ivory ban to save the elephant. Is any of your country's foreign aid earmarked for African wildlife conservation? You might want to find out, and insist that your tax dollars provide that sort of much-needed help.

Of course, you can't do it all alone. But there are organizations around the world dedicated to fighting for the African elephant and for Earth's other wild species. They need your support. At the end of this chapter I have provided a list of organizations you can join, or support. Although I have tried to make it as thorough a list as possible, I may have left out some groups. You may well find them yourself.

The job of saving the African elephant is far from done. If we want the elephant to survive — and, indeed, if we want it to thrive — we must be in it for the long haul. We must decide, in this "Deciding Decade," that the African elephant is worth that effort and that commitment.

At the beginning of this book, I said that we had a lesson to learn from the African elephant. We are learning about the ecological and socioeconomic role elephants play in Africa. We are learning that one species can attract money that can be used to save entire ecosystems. We are learning that we in the consumer nations hold the key to the markets for products like elephant ivory. The disappearance of those markets is teaching us that we have the power to make sweeping, positive changes.

Certainly the African elephant is safer now than it has been for decades. But if we assume the job is done and move on to other causes, the African countries will become cynical about our motives, and many of the gains we have made will, inevitably, be lost. We must follow through by helping African countries continue to preserve elephants and their ecosystems.

If we had failed to save the elephant, one of the world's most beloved animals, I'm not sure what we could have saved. However, the real lesson of the African elephant goes far beyond one species, one ecosystem or even one continent. The message of hope that our success thus far gives us should fire us for the infinitely greater and more complex task of saving the world that we and the elephants share. The African elephant has taught us that we can make a difference, and that we who care about the fate of this world must never give up.

ORGANIZATIONS WITH ELEPHANT-RELATED
CONSERVATION PROGRAMS

I have made no effort to rate the organizations on this list in any way. I encourage you to get in touch directly with any group you would like to support and ask for details on what, and how much, they are doing for elephants—and for Africa—*before* you write a check.

African Wildlife Conservation Fund, P.O. Box 627, Adelaide Stn., 36 Adelaide St. E., Toronto, Ont., M5C 2J8, Canada: supports elephant conservation projects in Kenya, Namibia and elsewhere; maintains a conservation, education and public awareness campaign in Canada.

African Wildlife Foundation, 1717 Massachusetts Ave., NW, Washington, D.C. 20036, USA: active in African wildlife conservation, with an office in Nairobi supplying field expertise, equipment, programs and scholarships; leads Elephant Awareness Campaign in the United States.

Animal Welfare Institute, P.O. Box 3650, Washington, D.C. 20007, USA: active anti-ivory campaign; supports investigative projects of Environmental Investigation Agency.

*Care for the Wild, 1 Ashfolds, Rusper, Horsham, West Sussex RH12 4QX, UK: co-founder of ELEFRIENDS; elephant adoption program with Daphne Sheldrick in Nairobi and Tsavo National Parks.

*David Sheldrick Wildlife Appeal, P.O. Box 15555, Nairobi, Kenya: memorial to Daphne Sheldrick's late husband, first warden of Tsavo National Park; supports Nairobi Elephant Orphanage, re-introduction of orphans to the wild, and antipoaching work in Kenya.

*East African Wildlife Society, P.O. Box 20110, Nairobi, Kenya: promotes wildlife conservation in Africa.

*ELEFRIENDS — The Elephant Protection Group, Cherry Tree Cottage, Coldharbour, Dorking, Surrey RH5 6HA, UK: umbrella organization for many groups; projects include ELE-TRUCK, a mobile repair workshop for antipoaching vehicles in Tanzania, and *Tusk I*, an anti-ivory-smuggling patrol boat, and creation of Petit Loanga, Gabon's first national park.

Environmental Investigation Agency, 208–209 Upper St., London, N1 1RL UK; 1506 19th St., NW, Washington, D.C. 20036, USA: undertook two-year undercover investigation of international ivory trade, with resulting exposé triggering British and European import bans; report on trade played critical role at 1989 CITES meeting; ongoing monitoring of ivory trade.

*Forsvara Elefanterna, Muskoten 30, S-14800 OSMO, Sweden: group similar to ELEFRIENDS.

Friends of Animals, P.O. Box 1244, Norwalk, Conn., 06856, USA: supplies motor vehicles to several African countries for antipoaching patrols; now restoring water supply, destroyed by siltation, for desert elephants in Gourma, Mali.

Greenpeace International, Keizersgracht 176, 1016 D.W., Amsterdam, The Netherlands: ongoing monitoring of illegal trade in ivory.

Bull elephants like this one in the Zambesi Valley, Zimbabwe, have more rounded foreheads than do cows. Both sexes of African elephant may have large tusks, unlike their Asian cousins.

Humane Society of the United States, 2100 L St., NW, Washington, D.C. 20037, USA: supports elephant conservation projects in Kenya and elsewhere; promotes boycott of ivory in the United States and worldwide; public awareness campaign; active CITES participation.

*International Wildlife Coalition, Holly Park, 634 North Falmouth Highway, North Falmouth, Mass., 62556, USA; IWC-Canada, P.O. Box 461, Port Credit Postal Station, Mississauga, Ont. L5G 4M1, Canada: scholarship program for children of Tanzanian game wardens; supports Daphne Sheldrick's elephant orphanage; active CITES involvement and anti-ivory campaign.

*Kenya Wildlife Fund, P.O. Box 2445, Stn. ''B,'' Richmond Hill, Ont., L4E 1A5, Canada: official representative of Kenya Wildlife Service in Canada; supports elephant conservation and habitat protection in Kenya; conducts public education campaign in Canada.

Nigerian Conservation Foundation, P.O. Box 467, Lagos, Nigeria: received funds from ELEFRIENDS to buy vehicle for Yankari Game Reserve.

Robin des Bois, 15 rue Ferdinand Duval, 75004 Paris, France: anti-ivory campaigns; promotes use of vegetable ivory — the hard seed of a South American palm — as a substitute product.

*Save the Rhino Trust, P.O. Box 22691, Windhoek 9000, Namibia: conservation of desert elephants.

*Société nationale de la protection de la nature, 57 rue Cuvier, 75005 Paris, France: co-sponsor, with Friends of Animals, of Amnistie pour les éléphants and Mali water-hole restoration program.

*Tusk Force, 1 Helix Gardens, London SW2 2JR, UK: sends vehicles to help antipoaching forces in Africa.

The calf, which struggles to its feet within minutes of its birth, is rarely far from its mother during its first few years. This mother and juvenile were photographed in Maasai Mara National Park, Kenya.

Wildlife Conservation International, New York Zoological Society, Bronx, N.Y. 10460, USA: overseas division of NYZS; sponsored Ivory Trade Review, which argued strongly for CITES ban; supports field research on forest elephants; monitors critical elephant populations at Amboseli National Park and elsewhere in Kenya and Tanzania; Nairobi office directed by David Western.

*Wildlife Conservation Society of Tanzania, P.O. Box 70919, Dar es Salaam, Tanzania: directs operations of ELE-TRUCK project for ELEFRIENDS.

World Wildlife Fund-U.S. 1250 Twenty-fourth St., NW, Washington, D.C. 20037, USA: monitors ivory trade; supports numerous field projects in Africa.

Zoocheck Canada, 5334 Yonge St., Suite 1830, Willowdale, Ont. M2N 6M2, Canada: maintains Kenya Wild Elephant Fund, supporting elephant conservation efforts in Kenya; sponsored 1989 conference, "Elephants: The Deciding Decade."

*These are participating organizations in the African Ele-Fund, a network of organizations channelling donations for practical conservation work in Africa. Only organizations with separate elephant-related projects are listed here; for a complete list of account holders, write: The African Ele-Fund, P.O. Box 308, Bristol BS99 7LQ, UK.

THE INTERNATIONAL WILDLIFE COALITION

The International Wildlife Coalition was launched in 1983, when four animal welfare and wildlife groups united into one international organization with a common goal: the protection of wild animals. We have offices in the United States, Canada, Brazil, Australia, Sri Lanka and the United Kingdom. Our mandate is to work across national boundaries to investigate and challenge excessive killing of and cruelty to wildlife, the destruction of wilderness, and the abuses of government agencies and commercial wildlife merchants.

Since its formation, the International Wildlife Coalition has accomplished a great deal. In Sri Lanka we have created a sanctuary to protect the nesting beaches of endangered sea turtles, and re-excavated clogged tanks to provide drinking water for the wildlife of the Yala National Park — including the rare Sri Lankan form of the Asian elephant. In the United States, our Whale Adoption Project has funded research and education projects on whales of the eastern seaboard. In 1991 the International Wildlife Coalition launched the *RV Navaho*, a specially-commissioned fifty-foot (15 m) vessel that will patrol the New England coast from the Gulf of Maine to Cape Cod, providing a base for whale research, marine mammal rescue operations and support for law enforcement officials seeking to protect marine life.

On the international scene, we have fought for legislative change to protect marine mammals, fur-bearers and other threatened creatures. One of our most important goals has been the end of the global ivory trade. As organizers of the African Elephant Emergency Network, we were successful in achieving a unilateral ban on ivory imports into Canada. We have been active at CITES, and played a key role in the fight to upgrade the African elephant to Appendix I. In 1992 IWC will send a delegation to the next CITES meeting in Japan, to continue the struggle for the African elephant and other exploited wildlife.

The International Wildlife Coalition is committed to helping Africa protect its elephants. We support Daphne Sheldrick's elephant orphanage in Kenya. The royalties from this book will go to our scholarship program for the children of game wardens in Tanzania, administered by Costa Mlay, Tanzania's Director of Wildlife.

Edward F. Brewer, Director of the Department of Wildlife Conservation in Gambia, has said, "By supporting the International Wildlife Coalition, you can personally manifest your practical concern for improving care and protection of the natural areas and wild animals that inhabit our threatened world."

149

*Individual elephants can
often be recognized by facial
features, ear shape or, as in
the case of a bull like the one
on the left, by asymmetry in
the position or size of the
tusks. These two were
photographed on Fothergill
Island, Zimbabwe, where the
local game wardens know,
and have names for, each of
the resident bulls.*

ACKNOWLEDGMENTS

PUTTING THIS BOOK TOGETHER INVOLVED A FLURRY OF FAXES, TELEPHONE CALLS, letters, cassette tapes and hand-delivered messages flying across four continents. At times, the task of locating my busy collaborators in Africa and elsewhere from my desk in Mississauga, Ontario, made me feel like an electronic Stanley in wireless pursuit of a whole series of Livingstones. It would all have been impossible without help, and fortunately I had plenty.

First, of course, I must express special gratitude to my collaborators, not only for their contribution to this book but for all they have done for the African elephant over the years. In particular, I must thank Ian Redmond, who really deserves credit as a co-editor as well as a contributor. Ian had a hand in the content and planning of the book, provided me with contacts and information, acted as a way station when fax messages failed to arrive from Africa, carried messages to Kenya and was a general source of encouragement and ideas. I must also thank Hezy Shoshani, who came into the planning of the book at a late date, but more than made up for it through his advice, encouragement and particularly his invaluable assistance in the preparation of the text for the picture captions and photo essays.

Rob Laidlaw and Holly Penfound of Zoocheck Canada deserve a special acknowledgment. In November 1989, Zoocheck staged "Elephants: The Deciding Decade," a massive event that packed Toronto's Convocation Hall and raised $140,000 for the Kenya Wildlife Service. Zoocheck Canada has kindly given permission to use *Elephants: The Deciding Decade* as the title of this book; the event provided its initial inspiration. As emcee for the evening, I was responsible for introducing some of the world's leading authorities on the African elephant, including Ian Redmond and Richard Leakey. It was excellent on-the-job training for this book, in which I am doing the same thing. Some of the material in these pages has been adapted from talks given at that event. Rob and Holly provided tape recordings of the evening, as well as willing ears and useful comments. The title itself was originally coined by my good friend Barry Kent Mackay.

ACKNOWLEDGMENTS

David Western's chapter was adapted from his 1989 Fairfield Osborn Memorial Lecture, presented to the New York Zoological Society. I am grateful to Geoffrey Mellor of Wildlife Conservation International for providing a tape recording of Dr. Western's talk and additional supporting material. Richard Leakey's chapter was based in part on a speech given in Nairobi in July 1990. Mwamba Shete of the East African Wildlife Society provided a cassette of the speech, and Lisa Abram brought it back from Kenya for me. I thank them both for their efforts.

Steven Best, Anne Doncaster and Donna Hart of the International Wildlife Coalition deserve my thanks not only for the help they gave me on this project, but also for giving me the opportunity, through IWC, to work on the elephant issue. The scholarship program in Tanzania that the royalties from this book will benefit was set up by Steve and Donna in collaboration with Costa Mlay, Tanzania's Director of Wildlife.

Pat Koval of the African Wildlife Conservation Fund and Dr. Susan Lieberman of the U.S. CITES Management Authority have been a great help with their comments and encouragement. Louise Charlton, founder of the Kenya Wildlife Fund and one of the organizers of "Elephants: The Deciding Decade," kindly chased down obscure details and hard-to-locate photographs. Bill Clark of Friends of Animals provided much useful, up-to-date information. Among the many people who helped me send and receive messages from my collaborators I would particularly like to thank Dr. Mark Stanley Price of the African Wildlife Foundation in Nairobi, and the staff of the Atrium Hotel, Darwin, Australia. I must also thank Laurie Coulter, who proved to be a diligent and cooperative editor.

The book you hold in your hand is only one of many possible books that could have been written about the African elephant. I have been fortunate in being able to present contributions by some of the most respected names in elephant biology and the conservation of African wildlife in general. But I cannot close these acknowledgments without paying tribute to some people who were not able, because of other commitments, to contribute to these pages. I must thank Iain and Oria Douglas-Hamilton, Cynthia Moss and Joyce Poole for their friendship and inspiration to a fellow-lobbyist at the 1989 CITES meeting and for their encouragement — and, particularly, that of Katherine Payne — during the early stages of the assembling of this book. More to the point, they deserve the thanks of all of us for their years of dedication to the African elephant and its survival.

R.O.

ABOUT THE CONTRIBUTORS

Brian Beck was born in Ottawa, and graduated from Carleton University. Always a wildlife enthusiast, he became fascinated by elephants while working with a young Asian elephant in a private game farm in western Canada. He moved east and spent the next six years working at the Metro Toronto Zoo with a herd of African elephants. Here he met his wife, Dr. Dale Smith, a wildlife veterinarian, and with her moved to Zimbabwe. He first picked up a camera while working in Hwange National Park on a research project concerning elephants, and for the next two years photographed wildlife throughout southern Africa. The couple then traveled north in a Land Rover and spent a further year exploring the parks and wilderness of the African continent. The elephants of seven African countries are represented in his collection. His photographs of wildlife have been published in books and calendars in Zimbabwe, Kenya and Canada. He currently lives in Guelph, Ontario, with his wife and daughter.

All photographs were taken with a Minolta X700 camera using Fujichrome film.

Richard Leakey was born in Nairobi, the son of archaeologists Drs. Louis and Mary Leakey. He has led many expeditions, including the famed "Origin of Man" excavations. Forgoing a formal university education, he became Administrative Director and later Chief Executive of the National Museums of Kenya. He has since received honorary degrees from several universities, as well as many prizes and awards. He serves as chairperson on the boards of several conservation and scientific organizations. Dr. Leakey has written numerous books and papers, and has taken part in many television documentaries. In April 1989, he was appointed Director of the Wildlife Conservation and Management Department for Kenya, recently transformed into a parastatal organization called the Kenya Wildlife Service.

Dr. Perez Olindo was Director of Kenya's Park Service from 1966 to 1976, Science Secretary of the National Council for Science and Technology, Kenya, in 1977–78, Chief Ecologist of the Lake (Victoria) Development Authority between 1980 and 1986, and Director of Wildlife and National Parks from 1987 to 1989. Dr. Olindo is presently a Senior Associate of the African Wildlife Foundation. He has the primary responsibility for coordinating AWF's African Elephant Conservation Programme and Policy. Since 1981, he has acted as expert consultant to the United Nations Environment Program, and in 1988 was elected to UNEP's Global 500 Honor Roll. In the same year, Dr. Olindo was the winner of the J. Paul Getty Conservation Prize. At the 1989 CITES meeting in Lausanne, Switzerland, he chaired the Working Group entrusted with drawing up the detailed rules governing the ivory trade ban. He lives in Nairobi, Kenya.

Ronald Orenstein, Project Director for the International Wildlife Coalition, holds a Ph.D. in Zoology from the University of Michigan and an LL.B. from the University of Toronto. He has represented IWC at the last two meetings of the Convention on International Trade in Endangered Species (CITES). At the 1987 meeting he acted as advisor to the delegation of Malaysia. At the 1989 meeting he was one of the engineers of the compromise amendment that led to an international ivory ban. In Canada, he was a coordinator of the African Elephant Emergency Network and acted as emcee for Zoocheck Canada's fundraising event, "Elephants: The Deciding Decade." Dr. Orenstein is a member of the Executive Council of Canadians for the Conservation of Tropical Nature, and of the Advisory Board of the Canadian Association for the United Nations Environment Program. He is also Chairman of the Scientific Advisory Council of Zoocheck Canada.

A wildlife biologist, lecturer and photojournalist, **Ian Redmond** completed a degree in biology with a minor in geology from the University of Keele, England. Between 1976 and 1983, he studied mountain gorillas in Rwanda and Zaire, cave elephants in Kenya, and reptiles and amphibians in Papua New Guinea. He appears regularly on radio and television, and serves as consultant in the making of television documentaries and feature movies, including *Gorillas in the Mist*. He is the Coordinator of the African Ele-Fund, the UK Representative of the Digit Fund (for gorilla research and conservation), a Fellow of the Zoological Society of London and an Honourary Research Associate of Hull University. He has published numerous books, articles and scientific papers, many of which have been translated into several languages. His next book will be *The Story of Digit*, a biography of the famous gorilla.

Dr. Jeheskel (Hezy) Shoshani's interest in nature started in Kibbutz Misgav-Am, Israel, where he established an Animal Corner and Natural History Museum. After five years at Tel-Aviv Zoo, where he rose to become Head Zookeeper, he became fascinated with elephants. In 1977 he established the Elephant Interest Group, an international non-profit organization, and has since edited its publication *Elephant*. He also acts as a consultant to the National Geographic Society. The author of over 50 publications, Dr. Shoshani has conducted research in natural history museums and at palaeontological sites worldwide, and directed the assemblies

Portrait of a bull in the Chobe National Park, Botswana.

of mastodon and Asian elephant skeletons now on display in Michigan. He has observed wild elephants in China and Kenya, including the "cave elephants" of Mount Elgon National Park, where he encountered Ugandan poachers. Dr. Shoshani lives near Detroit, Michigan, with his wife Sandra and Shafan, a rock hyrax which is, he says, the closest he could get to having an elephant as a house pet.

David Western is a Kenyan conservationist best known for his efforts to reconcile wildlife conservation with the interests of local people. His long-term efforts led to the creation of Amboseli National Park. He is deeply involved in conservation education programs as chairman of the Wildlife Clubs of Kenya and has, over the last decade, been in the forefront of efforts to conserve the African Elephant and Black Rhino. He is chairman of the African Elephant and Rhino Specialist Group of IUCN. He is former Director and currently Regional Director of Wildlife Conservation International.

FURTHER READING

A TREMENDOUS AMOUNT HAS BEEN, AND CONTINUES TO BE, WRITTEN ABOUT elephants. This list includes nineteen books, two articles, and one non-technical report, all published before the end of 1990.

Beard, P. H. *The End of the Game*. New York: Doubleday & Company, 1977. A history of the decline of African wildlife at European hands, with magnificent black-and-white photographs.

Buss, I. O. *Elephant Life: Fifteen Years at High Population Density*. Ames, Iowa: Iowa State University Press, 1990. A study of elephant ecology in Uganda during the 1950s and 1960s.

Carrington, R. *Elephants: A Short Account of Their Natural History, Evolution and Influence on Mankind*. London: Penguin, 1958. A classic, if dated, introduction to elephants.

Douglas-Hamilton, I., and O. Douglas-Hamilton. *Among the Elephants*. New York: Viking Press, 1975. An extraordinary account of a detailed field study of African elephants.

Douglas-Hamilton, O. *The Elephant Family Book*. Saxonville, Mass.: Picture Book Studios, 1990. A book for younger readers.

Eltringham, S. K. *Elephants*. Poole, Dorset: Blanford Press, 1982. A good account of elephant natural history.

Environmental Investigation Agency. *A System of Extinction: The African Elephant Disaster*. London: Environmental Investigation Agency, 1989. The ground-breaking exposé of the ivory trade, available from EIA.

Freeman, D. *Elephants: The Vanishing Giants*. New York: Putnam, 1981. An illustrated popular natural history of elephants.

Hanks, J. *The Struggle for Survival: The Elephant Problem*. New York: Mayflower Books, 1979. An account of the elephant crisis up to the late 1970s.

Ivory: An International History and Illustrated Survey. New York: Harry N. Abrams, 1987. Hardly a conservationist's choice — it is directed at ivory collectors — this is, nonetheless, a sumptuous and detailed account of man's infatuation with ivory.

Jackson, P. *Endangered Species — Elephants*. London: Quintet, 1990. An up-to-date account of elephant natural history, the history of elephants and man, and elephant conservation.

Kunkel, R. *Elephants*. New York: Harry N. Abrams, 1982. A magnificent collection of elephant photographs.

Moss, C. *Elephant Memories: Thirteen Years in the Life of An Elephant Family*. New York: William Morrow, 1988. A heartfelt and fascinating account of the lives of Amboseli's elephants.

Nichol, J. *The Animal Smugglers*. New York: Facts on File, 1987. A general account of the worldwide illegal trade in wildlife and wildlife products, including ivory.

Parker, I. and M. Amin. *Ivory Crisis*. London: Chatto & Windus, 1983. The elephant crisis as seen from the point of view of a spokesman for the ivory traders.

Payne, K. "Elephant Talk." *National Geographic* 176 (August 1989): 264–277. An article on the discovery of the "secret" language of elephants.

Poole, J. H. "Elephants in Musth, Lust." *Natural History* 96 (November 1987): 47–55. A fascinating article on the elephant's drive to reproduce.

Redmond, I. *The Elephant Book*. London: Walker Books, 1990. A brief, well-illustrated plea for the survival of the African elephant, suitable for younger, as well as aldult, readers.

Sheldrick, D. *An Elephant Called Eleanor*. London: Dent, 1981. The story of an orphaned baby elephant and its human foster parent, whose elephant orphanage is world-famous.

Sikes, S. K. *The Natural History of the African Elephant*. London: Weidenfeld and Nicolson, 1971. A classic reference book.

Williams, H. *Sacred Elephant*. London: Jonathan Cape, 1989. A celebration of elephants in pictures and quotations.

Wilson, D. and P. Ayerst. *White Gold*. New York: Taplinger, 1976. A history of the ivory trade and its role in Africa.

INDEX

Will elephants of the future be elusive and shy, fleeing from man like this herd of cows in South Africa's Addo National Park?